Published by Familius LLC, www.familius.com

Familius books are available at special discounts for bulk purchases for sales promotions, family
or corporate use. Special editions, including personalized covers, excerpts of existing books,
or books with corporate logos, can be created in large quantities for special needs. For more
information, contact Premium Sales at 559-876-2170 or email specialmarkets@familius.com.

Library of Congress Catalog-in-Publication Data

2015941461
ISBN 9781942672920

Cover and book design by David Miles
Edited by Liza Hagerman

10 9 8 7 6 5 4 3 2 1

First Edition

Printed in China

CHIA CRAZY

CLEAN EATING
···· with the ····
WORLD'S GREATEST SUPER FOOD

BRITNEY RULE & CHERIE SCHETSELAAR

FAMILIUS

AUTHOR'S NOTE

. . . .

My name is Britney, and Cherie is my mom. Food is intuitive for my mom. She can make bread or muffins without consulting a recipe. When she began changing recipes on her own to make them healthier, that started to be a problem. No one could replicate what she was making. Sometimes even she couldn't replicate what she had made to her satisfaction.

So I encouraged her to start a blog, and I promised to help her. This journey has evolved into the books *Grain Crazy* and *Quinoa Crazy* and then into this book—all about the wonderful superfood chia. And we're not only crazy about chia, but we're also crazy about helping people eat healthier. We hope the recipes in this book provide an easy and healthful way to incorporate this beautiful food into your diet.

—*Britney Rule*

CONTENTS

CHIA 101

WHAT IS CHIA?

Chia is a small black, white, purple, brown, or mottled seed that comes from a variety of flowering mint plant, but you might know it best from the popular '80s infomercial selling terracotta figures that grow leafy hair. They are actually the same plant! Recently, chia has become a favorite food fad that you can find in snacks, drinks, and crackers in any store. Why has chia become so popular?

- It's packed full of nutrients, such as omega-3 fatty acids, magnesium, iron, calcium, potassium, vitamin A, manganese, and phosphorus, and it's a substantial source of fiber, protein, and antioxidants.

- It's incredibly easy to use as a supplement in foods you and your family already eat, adding a boost of nutrition without changing your eating habits.

- Chia can help you feel full longer, which may promote weight loss. This is partly because of its high fiber content and because it's a great source of protein, but it's also because it gels when water is added. The gel it forms is digested more slowly than other foods and helps you feel full longer. Although research on the topic is still in its early stages, chia is also believed to boost energy.

CHIA'S HEALTH BENEFITS

Chia doesn't have magical powers, but it is legitimately a superfood that can add powerful nutrients to the foods you eat. What is a superfood? It's an especially nutrient-dense food—high in vitamins and minerals and low in sugars, unhealthy fats, and additives—that is considered especially good for your health. Think of using chia as an easy way to increase the variety of vitamins and nutrients you eat—a health supplement in a beautiful little seed.

OMEGA-3 FATTY ACIDS: Chia has an unusually high content of omega-3s, essential fatty acids that cannot be made by our bodies. Omega-3s benefit your heart and brain, and they make it easier for your body to absorb the vitamin D needed for healthy bones and teeth. These amazing essential fats also reduce triglyceride levels, lowering the risk of heart disease.

FIBER: There are 10 grams of fiber in every 2 tablespoons of chia. Considering the recommended daily amount of fiber is 25–30 grams, chia helps you get there easily. Fiber is beneficial in reducing total cholesterol and LDL cholesterol (the bad kind). A high fiber content plus omega-3s and alpha-linolenic acid, which chia also contains, make chia especially beneficial in lowering cholesterol levels.

PROTEIN: In only a 2-tablespoon serving, chia contains 4.4 grams of protein. A large egg (about 4 tablespoons) has approximately 6 grams of protein. Not only is chia's protein high for such a small serving size, but it also contains every essential amino acid, making it a complete protein in the same way that meat or dairy is. This makes chia a great vegetarian protein source.

CALCIUM: Calcium is important for bone and tooth health, and chia is a significant source. A serving of chia contains 17 percent of the recommended daily intake. Also, chia contains boron and magnesium, which aid in the absorption of calcium.

MAGNESIUM: Chia contains 24 percent of your daily recommended amount of magnesium in 2 tablespoons. Magnesium aids in the absorption of calcium, and it has been shown to lower the risk of heart attacks when taken in high doses.

ANTIOXIDANTS: Chia is a great source of antioxidants—even more than blueberries! Interestingly, the antioxidants also help chia have a longer shelf life despite its high oil content.

OTHER MINERALS: Chia is also a good source of iron, potassium, phosphorus, and manganese, which are all important to human life.

GLUTEN-FREE: This means chia fits into nearly everyone's diets. Also, since American foods are often loaded with excess gluten, it can be beneficial to add a food without gluten to your diet.

GLYCEMIC INDEX: Chia has a very low glycemic index value, meaning that it doesn't spike your blood sugar and can even help slow down the absorption of other carbs, preventing the sugar highs and lows of carb-heavy foods.

BEFORE THE RECENT FAD

Chia is native to Central America and is frequently found in foods and drinks in Mexico, Guatemala, Paraguay, Bolivia, and Argentina. The word "chia" comes from the Mayan word *chiabaan*, which means "strengthening," and the Aztec word *chian*, which means "oily."

Chia has been used and revered by several ancient civilizations, such as the Mayans, Aztecs, and Tehuantepecs. They used it for food and for medicine, and the Aztecs even used chia seeds as a form of money. Some historians believe it was as important of a crop as corn to the Aztec people. The Mayan people used chia in ceremonial drinks.

Chia in America has outgrown the Chia Pet® in recent years as people have begun to discover the nutrients it contains and have started to incorporate it into their diets.

HOW DO I USE CHIA?

Chia is so easy to use! Because it has little flavor on its own, you can add it to many different types of foods you are already eating, which makes it an ideal solution for increasing the amount of vitamins and nutrients we come in contact with daily. And you don't need very much to get the full benefits listed earlier. Here are some of our favorite ways to eat chia:

PUDDING

Since chia is a great thickener, it makes a delicious pudding without as much sweetener. Chia seeds create a pudding similar to tapioca in texture when mixed with milk and sweetener and can be made any flavor. Ground chia can also be used to thicken food without the texture of the seeds.

SEEDS OR NUTS

In any recipe, when you use seeds or nuts, add a scoop of chia seeds along with them. Cooked or raw, they will give your dish a nutrition boost.

EGG REPLACEMENT

Mix 3 tablespoons of water and 1 tablespoon of ground chia and let it sit for 5–10 minutes until a thick gel forms. This makes a substitute for 1 egg that can be used in baking, even in cookies and cakes.

SOUPS AND SAUCES

Again, chia is an excellent thickener. Add the seeds to soups or sauces where you would normally add a spoonful of flour or cornstarch. If the textures don't match, blend the chia before adding it for a smoother finish.

SALAD DRESSINGS

Salad dressings often benefit from a little thicker consistency so they don't just slide off your lettuce and vegetables. Chia seeds will thicken your dressings—add a tablespoon or two.

BREADS

Add 1/3 cup of chia seeds to your bread or muffin dough, or roll the dough in chia seeds after it is formed, just as you would with sesame seeds.

SMOOTHIES

Add 1 tablespoon per serving of chia seeds to your favorite smoothie.

PREPARING CHIA

GRIND IT INTO A POWDER. Chia can be ground and added to food in powder form. This works especially well when using it as a thickener. You may also be able to find ground chia at your local store. If not, you can grind it yourself in a coffee grinder. Do not put it in a grain grinder, since chia's high level of oil can clog the grinder. Ground or whole, chia retains the same nutritional benefits.

MAKE IT INTO A GEL. Chia can absorb a lot of water. To make a chia gel, add 4 tablespoons of water to 1 tablespoon of chia. Let it sit for at least 5–10 minutes, then leave it in the refrigerator until you're ready to add it to your favorite drinks.

CLEAN EATING 101

WHY EAT CLEAN?

In writing this book about chia, we've chosen to make the recipes in this book clean because we believe that eating pure, unprocessed foods in all food groups is the best way to have a diet that is sustainable long term (by diet we mean the foods you eat, not a weight loss plan) and will provide the best benefits for your health. We believe in feeling good! And we feel that eating a variety of whole grains, fruits, vegetables, dairy, and even some meats is the best way to get a balanced mix of nutrients and vitamins and to feel your best.

HOW TO EAT CLEAN

The term "clean eating" is always subject to interpretation, but here are some of the principles to which we try to aspire:

AVOID PROCESSED FOODS. This is the basic tenet of healthy eating. A lot of the foods we eat are processed to some degree. Cooking your meat involves processing it, and I think most of us wouldn't want to eat all of our meat raw—plus, clean eating is not a raw diet. But many processed foods contain large amounts of salt and calories, and they often contain refined sugar and carbohydrates as well as colorings and unhealthy additives.

But not all processed foods are bad for you. How do you know which ones are? Read the ingredient list on packaged foods! If you don't recognize the ingredients, or the ingredients aren't something you would keep in your kitchen, chances are good that you've found a food that is probably more processed than is best for you. You are able to make choices about just how processed you are willing to eat. We, for example, use rinsed canned beans in many of our recipes. Some people may feel that only dried beans are truly "clean," but we think that if you are able to find a brand that is low in sodium or, better yet, canned in just water, then canned beans can have a healthful place in your diet. You can make similar judgment calls about your own food.

EAT WHOLE GRAINS. White flour is a pretty big no-no in clean eating. Instead of using white flour, which has nearly no natural nutrients, you should use whole grains that provide you with substantial health benefits.

CUT DOWN ON ALL SWEETENER USAGE. Nearly everyone would benefit from reducing the sugar in their diet. Our muffins taste like muffins, not cupcakes, and we also choose not to use white sugar—we instead use honey and cut down on all our sugar usage.

EAT MORE FRUITS AND VEGETABLES. The best way to get a variety of nutrients in your diet is to eat a variety of fruits and vegetables. We try to make fruits and vegetables a large part of our diet and our recipes.

EAT PROTEIN REGULARLY, BUT CUT DOWN ON MEAT. There are so many wonderful sources of protein (Hello, chia!) that don't include meat. We try to use beans, nuts, and seeds more frequently, but we don't cut out meat entirely. We believe that moderation is healthy.

EAT HEALTHY FATS. Your body needs fat to operate, but make an effort to eat the healthy kinds. We try to use healthy oils, such as coconut, olive, and grapeseed oil. We also love the natural fats found in avocados, salmon, flaxseed, and chia.

DRINK TO YOUR HEALTH. Avoid drinking your calories with low-nutrient, high-calorie beverages. Drink water most of the time.

BUY ORGANIC AND LOCAL. Whenever possible, it is best to buy foods that are organic, local, and sustainably grown. Organic and local food is often cost prohibitive for some budgets but is best to eat when possible. Try to buy meats from grass- and range-fed animals as well as eggs from free-range chickens.

There are different schools of thought on clean eating, but that is ours. The recipes you find in our books will follow these principles.

TIPS FOR EATING CLEAN

PLAN. Clean eating is hard to do in a hurry. Plan out your meals so you don't scramble to get food ready and succumb to processed food out of hunger.

MAKE SNACKS AHEAD OF TIME. One of the hardest times to eat clean is when snacking. Plan out your snacks ahead of time and put them easy-to-grab containers for on-the-go eating. Many of our snack recipes freeze well, allowing you to make a big batch in advance and eat the snacks as you need them.

STOP BUYING THE ALTERNATIVE. If you don't have processed food in the house, you can't eat it! Processed food sitting on your shelf is sometimes hard to ignore when you're short on time, hungry, or just feeling snack-y.

START AT YOUR OWN PACE. If this sort of diet is new and overwhelming to you, you may do well to start one step at a time. Pick one meal to change, or concentrate on snacks for starters. Any step forward is good, and if you're not used to eating whole grains and vegetables frequently, it might take a little while for your body to adjust.

DON'T BEAT YOURSELF UP OVER "FAILURES." Eating healthy is a process, and it's something you do for your own benefit. So if you have a bad day of eating, or even a week, don't give yourself a hard time. You can always recommit to eating well.

MAKE YOUR OWN. The sauces, dressings, and spreads in the store often have many additives that aren't good for you, but you can make your own versions. Do you crave barbecue sauce? Make a big batch of homemade sauce and store the extra in your freezer. In love with a specific salad dressing? Look for a version made from scratch online. Your homemade versions will be healthier and will likely taste better, too.

BREAK FAST

PUMPKIN CHIA OATMEAL

THIS OATMEAL IS ONE OF OUR FAVORITE BREAKFASTS, THOUGH IT ALSO MAKES A HEALTHY SNACK OR LUNCH. THE ADDED CHIA IS A GREAT SHOT OF NUTRITION TO START THE DAY, AND WHILE PUMPKIN IS OFTEN THOUGHT OF AS AN AUTUMN FOOD, WE FIND IT TO BE A COMFORT-FOOD FLAVOR FOR ANY TIME OF YEAR. THIS RECIPE CAN BE MADE THE NIGHT BEFORE ENJOYING OR QUICKLY FOR A MEAL ON THE GO.

INGREDIENTS

1 cup almond milk

1/3 cup old-fashioned oats

3 tablespoons chia seeds

2 teaspoons honey (or more if you want the oatmeal to be sweeter)

2 tablespoons 100 percent pure canned pumpkin puree

1/4 teaspoon cinnamon

Dash of nutmeg

2 tablespoons dark chocolate chips (70 percent cocoa or greater), crushed

Extra almond milk for topping (optional)

SERVES 2

1 Pour all the ingredients except the chocolate chips and almond milk for topping into a small airtight container and stir until ingredients are mixed. Place the mixture in the refrigerator for at least 2 hours to thicken.

2 Remove the mixture from the refrigerator, sprinkle with chocolate chips, and drizzle optional almond milk on top.

TIP:

We love to use fresh nutmeg, since it makes the pumpkin spice more pronounced. Purchase whole nutmegs from your local grocery store and use a zester to grate a bit of your own ground nutmeg.

BERRY GOOD MUESLI

FOOD HAS THE POTENTIAL TO BRING BACK SWEET MEMORIES. MOM USED TO MAKE THIS MUESLI FOR OUR FAMILY WHEN MY SIBLINGS AND I WERE CHILDREN, BACK WHEN SHE WASN'T FAMILIAR WITH CHIA. NOW WE CAN ENJOY IT AND REMINISCE AGAIN, BUT WITH AN ADDED NUTRITION BOOST!

1 Mix the yogurt, oats, chia, and honey together in a small bowl. Cover and store in the refrigerator overnight. If you don't have time, you can skip the overnight wait and instead let the mixture soak for 15 minutes in the refrigerator.

2 Remove the mixture from the refrigerator. Fold in the strawberries, blueberries, and banana and enjoy.

INGREDIENTS

2/3 cup plain yogurt

1/3 cup old-fashioned oats

2 tablespoons chia seeds

2 teaspoons honey or sweetener of your choosing

3 or 4 strawberries, chopped

1/4 cup blueberries

1/2 banana, sliced

SERVES 2

DID YOU KNOW?

Not only does soaking the oats in this recipe eliminate the need for cooking them, but there is also some evidence that soaking oats overnight in yogurt, milk, or water (before eating them) reduces the amount of phytic acid in the oats. Phytic acid can block nutrient absorption in the gut, so removing as much of the acid as possible will help your body retain more nutrients.

STEEL-CUT OATS

WITH TOASTED ALMONDS, COCONUT, AND RASPBERRIES

THIS CEREAL IS A FLAVORFUL TWIST ON OATMEAL. THE TOPPINGS WOULD BE YUMMY WITH YOGURT AS WELL. HAVING HOT CEREAL FOR BREAKFAST IS ONE OF MY FAVORITE WAYS TO START THE DAY OFF RIGHT. WHILE RASPBERRIES ARE DELICIOUS, YOU CAN ADD WHATEVER KIND OF BERRY IS CURRENTLY IN SEASON.

INGREDIENTS

2/3 cup steel-cut oats

1 cup water

2 tablespoons ground flaxseed

1/4 cup almond milk

1 tablespoon plus 2 teaspoons honey

1/2 cup unsweetened coconut flakes

1/3 cup chopped almonds

1 teaspoon coconut oil

Dash of salt

1/3 cup raspberries

2 tablespoons chia seeds

Almond milk for topping (optional)

SERVES 2–3

1. If possible, soak the oats the night before in water. For a quicker method, simply put the water and oats in a pot on medium-high heat and let them come to a boil.

2. Turn down the heat to medium-low. Stir in the flaxseed, almond milk, and 1 tablespoon of honey. Let the mixture cook until the oats are softened, stirring occasionally.

3. While the oats are cooking, pour the coconut flakes into a separate skillet on low heat and toast until the flakes reach a golden color. Remove the toasted coconut flakes from the skillet and set them aside.

4. Pour the almonds, coconut oil, 1 teaspoon of honey, and salt into the hot skillet. Toast the nuts until they are light brown. Remove the toasted nuts from the skillet and set them aside.

5. Pour the raspberries into the hot skillet with the remaining teaspoon of honey and the chia. Stir until the mixture starts to thicken. Take the mixture off the heat and set aside.

6. Pour the oats into bowls. Top with the raspberries, almonds, and then the coconut flakes. Pour almond milk on top, if desired.

OATMEAL KAMUT® WAFFLES

ENJOYING THESE WAFFLES IS A GREAT WAY TO START OFF A MORNING. THEY ARE LOADED WITH LOTS OF DELICIOUS GRAINS THAT WILL FILL YOU UP FAST AND GIVE YOU A BOOST OF ENERGY. HAVING A HEALTHY BREAKFAST IS ESSENTIAL TO HELPING YOUR OVERALL ENERGY LEVEL STAY HIGH FOR THE DAY. I FREEZE THE LEFTOVER WAFFLES AND THEN POP THEM IN THE TOASTER FOR MY BOYS WHEN THEY WANT A QUICK BREAKFAST OR SNACK.

INGREDIENTS

1 cup old-fashioned oats

2 tablespoons ground flaxseed

2 tablespoons ground chia seeds

2 1/4 cups almond milk

1 1/3 cups Kamut® flour

1 tablespoon baking powder

1 teaspoon cinnamon

1/4 teaspoon ground nutmeg (optional)

1/8 teaspoon salt

2 tablespoons honey (or more if you want sweeter waffles)

3 tablespoons grapeseed oil or coconut oil

Fresh or frozen fruit or jam for toppings

1 Heat a waffle iron.

2 In a medium bowl, pour the oats, flaxseed, chia, and almond milk. Stir gently to combine ingredients. Let the mixture sit about 5 minutes while you gather the remaining ingredients.

3 Add the flour, baking powder, cinnamon, nutmeg, salt, honey, and oil. Stir until ingredients are just combined. Let the batter sit another 5 minutes so that it expands.

4 Grease the waffle iron with a small amount of oil. Pour on the batter and cook. Serve hot with the buttermilk syrup and your other favorite toppings.

MAKES 12 WAFFLES

HONEY BUTTERMILK SYRUP

1 In a saucepan on medium-low heat, pour in the butter, buttermilk, and honey. Let the mixture come to a boil for 2 minutes.

2 Take mixture off heat. Stir in baking soda, vanilla, and optional almond extract.

INGREDIENTS

3 tablespoons butter

1/2 cup buttermilk

1/2 cup honey

1/2 teaspoon baking soda

1/2 teaspoon vanilla

2 teaspoons almond extract (optional, but recommended)

23

VEGGIE SCRAMBLE

WHILE THIS DISH IS DEFINITELY BREAKFAST APPROPRIATE, IT IS A DELICIOUS LUNCH AS WELL.

INGREDIENTS

1 egg

1 tablespoon chia seeds

1 1/2 tablespoons olive oil

2–3 mini bell peppers or 1 large bell pepper, chopped

1 tablespoon chopped onion

5 cherry tomatoes, chopped

Salt and pepper to taste

Salsa for garnish (homemade is best)

SERVES 1

1 In a small bowl, beat together the egg and chia. Set the bowl aside.

2 Heat the olive oil in a small frying pan on medium heat. Add the peppers, onion, and tomatoes. Sauté for 3–5 minutes until soft, stirring occasionally.

3 Stir the egg mixture into the vegetables. Cook until the eggs are to your preference.

4 Take the mixture off heat. Scoop onto to a plate, add salt and pepper, top with your favorite salsa, and enjoy.

WHOLE GRAIN PANCAKES

MOM IS PICKY ABOUT PANCAKES. THEY HAVE TO HAVE SOME MOISTNESS TO THEM WHILE STILL BEING LIGHT AND AIRY. THESE PANCAKES FIT HER REQUIREMENTS PERFECTLY.

1 Heat a griddle to about 300 degrees.

2 Mix all the dry ingredients in a bowl. Stir together with a wire whisk.

3 In a separate small bowl, combine the eggs, oil, honey, and milk and stir.

4 Combine the wet and dry ingredients. Stir until just mixed.

5 Grease the griddle with a small amount of oil. Pour the batter onto the griddle. Cook until pancakes are light golden on both sides.

6 Top with your favorite topping. We love them with homemade jam.

INGREDIENTS

2 cups whole grain flour

2 teaspoons baking powder

1/4 teaspoon salt

1 teaspoon cinnamon

2 tablespoons chia seeds

2 eggs

2 tablespoons olive oil

2 tablespoons honey

1 1/2 cups unsweetened almond milk

Your favorite pancake topping

MAKES ABOUT 10 PANCAKES

TIP:

We used spelt flour in this recipe. Spelt is similar to wheat but has a nutty taste, has less gluten, and is easier to digest. It's a wonderful, light whole grain flour that substitutes well in many recipes.

POMEGRANATE BREAKFAST BOWL

THE POMEGRANATE SEEDS IN THIS BREAKFAST BOWL ADD NUTRITION, COLOR, AND NATURAL SWEETNESS. WE LOVE THAT THIS MEAL IS LOADED WITH NUTRIENTS AND WILL GET YOU POWERED UP FOR YOUR DAY. YOU CAN ALSO ENJOY IT AS A SNACK FOR AN EXTRA POWER BOOST. YOU CAN USE THE RAW GRANOLA RECIPE ON PAGE 77, IF DESIRED.

INGREDIENTS

1 cup plain yogurt or plain Greek yogurt

3–4 tablespoons pomegranate seeds

1 tablespoon chia seeds

1/4 cup granola

2 tablespoons chopped dark chocolate chips (70 percent cocoa or greater) (optional)

Extra pomegranate seeds, grated chocolate chips, chia seeds, and granola for toppings

SERVES 1

1 Spoon the yogurt into a bowl and add the pomegranate seeds, chia, granola, and chocolate chips. Stir until all ingredients are combined.

2 Garnish with desired toppings.

BREAKFAST FRUIT FOOL

WE RECENTLY LEARNED ABOUT AN ENGLISH DESSERT CALLED "FRUIT FOOL." IT USUALLY CONSISTS OF FRUIT FOLDED INTO CUSTARD OR WHIPPED CREAM. MOM DECIDED TO RECREATE THE RECIPE AS A BREAKFAST USING WHIPPED COCONUT CREAM. THERE IS NO ADDED SUGAR—JUST ENJOY THE NATURAL SWEETNESS OF THE FRUIT.

1 Combine the kiwi, banana, lime juice, lime zest, and mangoes in a bowl. Stir them so that the juice covers all the fruit. (You could also puree the mangoes, if desired. Fruit fool is often made with fruit puree.) Stir in the chia and set the bowl aside.

2 Place the whipped coconut cream into a separate medium bowl. Add the vanilla and stir to combine.

3 Fold the fruit mixture into the cream. Scoop the mixture into dishes. Garnish with additional fruit, if desired, and enjoy.

INGREDIENTS

1 kiwi, peeled and chopped into bite-sized pieces

1 banana, sliced

2 tablespoons lime juice

1 teaspoon lime zest

1 cup chopped mangoes

2 tablespoons chia seeds

1/4 cup whipped coconut cream

1 teaspoon vanilla

Extra kiwis and mangoes, chopped, for toppings

SERVES 2

TIP:
To make the whipped coconut cream, chill a can of coconut milk for at least 5 hours in your refrigerator. After it has chilled, scoop the thickened milk off the top. Do not use the liquid on the bottom. Whip up the cream with a mixer or blender just as you would with regular whipped cream.

DRINKS & SMOOTHIES

STRAWBERRY KIWI SMOOTHIE

WE LOVE IT WHEN STRAWBERRIES ARE IN SEASON! THIS REFRESHING SMOOTHIE CAN TAKE ON AN ICE CREAM TEXTURE IF YOU CUT DOWN THE MILK TO A CUP AND A HALF AND PUT THE SMOOTHIE MIXTURE IN THE FREEZER TO THICKEN. YOU COULD ALSO ADD A HANDFUL OF SPINACH FOR EXTRA NUTRIENTS.

INGREDIENTS

2 cups almond milk

1 tablespoon honey (optional)

2 kiwis, peeled

2 tablespoons chia seeds

2 cups frozen strawberries

1 banana, chopped and frozen

SERVES 2

1 Pour all the ingredients into a blender in the order listed and pulse until smooth.

2 Enjoy immediately or store in the freezer to thicken.

DID YOU KNOW?

Aguas frescas are South and Central American drinks made with sugar and water and flavored with fruits, cereals, flowers, or seeds. (Horchata, anyone?) Chia is commonly used in these drinks, especially in vegetable-flavored ones.

BLUEBERRY CREAM DREAM

BLUEBERRIES CONTAIN A LARGE AMOUNT OF ANTIOXIDANTS, VITAMIN K, MANGANESE, AND VITAMIN C. THEY ARE ALSO LOW ON THE GLYCEMIC INDEX. AS A RESULT, THEY ARE FANTASTIC TO EAT ON A REGULAR BASIS. THIS SMOOTHIE MAKES ENJOYING THEM FREQUENTLY BOTH EASY AND DELICIOUS.

1 Pour all ingredients into a blender in the order listed and pulse until smooth.

2 Serve immediately.

INGREDIENTS

1 cup unsweetened vanilla almond milk

1 tablespoon chia seeds

1 banana, chopped and frozen

1 cup frozen blueberries

SERVES 2

TIP:

Should you chop up your bananas before you blend them? Although it may seem unnecessary, frozen whole bananas are hard on a blender's motor. Chopping them before blending them into your smoothie will prolong the life of your blender.

SUMMER FRUIT FRAPPÉ

WE LOVE SUMMERTIME. EVERYTHING ABOUT ENJOYING THE WATER, WARM WEATHER, SUMMER NIGHTS, SUMMER FRUIT, AND PLAYING WITH FAMILY AT THE LAKE ARE WONDERFUL. THIS YUMMY DRINK COMBINES MANY FRUITS WITH SPINACH TO GIVE YOU THE ENERGY YOU NEED FOR ALL YOUR SUMMER ACTIVITIES.

INGREDIENTS

1 cup water or almond milk

Juice from 1 orange

3 tablespoons yogurt

1 cup spinach

2 tablespoons chia seeds

1 tablespoon flaxseed

1 cup fresh or frozen pineapple chunks

1/2 cup fresh or frozen mango pieces

1/2 cup fresh or frozen peach slices

2 bananas, chopped and frozen

1/2 cup frozen blueberries or other berries

1 cup ice cubes

1 Pour the water or milk into a blender and then add all remaining ingredients in the order listed. Blend until smooth.

2 Serve and enjoy a refreshing power drink. It's great for a summer day!

SERVES 3–4

MANGO TANGO

WE LIKE TO RELY ON THE NATURAL SWEETNESS OF FRUIT WHENEVER WE CAN IN OUR RECIPES. THIS SMOOTHIE IS A REFRESHING AND DELICIOUS AFTERNOON SNACK THAT IS NATURALLY SWEET. YOU WILL LOVE IT!

1 Pour all ingredients into a blender in the order listed and pulse until smooth.

2 Serve immediately.

INGREDIENTS

1 cup almond milk

Juice from 1 orange

1 apple, core removed and peel left on

2 tablespoons chia seeds

1 handful of spinach

1 cup chopped frozen mangoes

1 1/2 bananas, chopped and frozen

SERVES 2

TIP:
For best results, always pack your blender with the liquids first, then the solids, and then the frozen items last. This will help your blender mix the ingredients more evenly.

PROTEIN-POWERED FRUIT SMOOTHIE

COTTAGE CHEESE HAS A WHOPPING TWELVE GRAMS OF PROTEIN IN JUST A HALF CUP. MOM DECIDED TO ADD IT TO A SMOOTHIE, AND IT BLENDS SMOOTHLY FOR A PERFECT PROTEIN BOOST. THIS SMOOTHIE HAS NO ADDED SUGAR.

INGREDIENTS

3 cups water

1/2 cup low-fat cottage cheese

1 large handful of spinach

2 tablespoons chia seeds

2 tablespoons flaxseed

1 cup frozen mango chunks

1/3 cup frozen blueberries

1/3 cup frozen raspberries

1/3 cup frozen peach slices

1/2 banana, chopped and frozen

SERVES 4

1 Pour the ingredients into a blender in the order listed.

2 Blend and stir, continuing until the mixture is creamy and smooth. Enjoy immediately.

DID YOU KNOW?

We all know the Chia Pet® jingle. Did you know that about 500,000 Chia Pets® are sold in the United States each year?

FRUIT-INFUSED WATER

FRUIT-INFUSED WATER IS PRIMARILY GREAT FOR HYDRATION, AND SOME NUTRITIONISTS ESTIMATE THAT WHEN YOU INFUSE WATER, YOU GET AS MUCH AS 20 PERCENT OF THE VITAMINS FOUND IN FRESHLY-SQUEEZED FRUIT JUICE WITHOUT THE ADDED CALORIES OR FRUCTOSE. THINK OF IT AS NATURAL VITAMIN WATER!

1 Place the lemon slices in a 1-quart mason jar and then add the other fruit on top. Put in the mint leaves and chia last.

2 Cover with water and place the jar in your refrigerator. Let it sit for about 4 hours in the refrigerator and enjoy within the next 3 days.

3 As you drink the water, add more water to your jar when the jar is only half full. That way, you can enjoy more infused water, and as the fruit loses its potency, the unflavored water will be mixed with the flavored water and keep more flavor.

INGREDIENTS

1/2 lemon, peeled and thinly sliced

6–8 strawberries, sliced in half

5–6 raspberries

1/4 cup blueberries, sliced in half

1/4 orange or lime, peeled and thinly sliced (optional)

5 mint leaves, ripped just a little to let out the flavor

1 tablespoon chia seeds

Water

Ice

TIP:

For a crowd, you could increase the ingredients and pour it into a glass pitcher. Fruit-infused water would make a beautiful drink for a party or gathering.

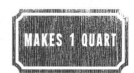

MAKES 1 QUART

BERRY HEMP BREAKFAST SMOOTHIE

HEMP IS A GREAT SOURCE OF OMEGA-3 FATTY ACIDS AND IS A COMPLETE PROTEIN BECAUSE IT CONTAINS ALL ESSENTIAL AMINO ACIDS—JUST LIKE MEAT, EGGS, AND DAIRY. WHEN THE WEATHER GETS TOO HOT TO TURN ON THE OVEN, WE OFTEN ENJOY A HEARTY SMOOTHIE LIKE THIS FOR DINNER, ESPECIALLY PAIRED WITH SOME VEGGIES.

INGREDIENTS

1/2 cup water

2 oranges, peeled and sectioned

1 cup spinach

1 tablespoon hemp seeds

2 tablespoons chia seeds

1 tablespoon flaxseed

1/4 cup frozen raspberries

1/2 cup frozen blueberries

1 banana, chopped and frozen

SERVES 2

1 Pour all the ingredients into a blender in the order listed and let the mixture whirl until nice and creamy.

2 Serve immediately and enjoy!

CREAMY MELON SLUSHIE

WE HAD NEVER THOUGHT ABOUT USING HONEYDEW MELONS IN A SLUSHIE UNTIL MOM TRIED ONE IN HAWAII. SHE LOVED IT SO MUCH THAT SHE WANTED TO MAKE ONE WHEN SHE GOT HOME. BELOW IS THE BEAUTY SHE CAME UP WITH. FOR THE BEST SLUSHIE TEXTURE, FREEZE THE CHOPPED MELON THE NIGHT BEFORE.

1 Combine the melon, honey, chia, and spinach in a blender. Blend until smooth. If your melon is especially sweet, you will not need as much honey.

2 Pour the ice cubes into the blender and pulse a couple of times, leaving small chunks of ice.

3 Divide into cups and serve immediately.

INGREDIENTS

1 1/2 cups chopped honeydew melon

1–2 tablespoons honey or sweetener of your choosing

3 tablespoons chia seeds

1 cup spinach

4 cups ice cubes

SERVES 2

DID YOU KNOW?

Honeydew melon contains some great nutrients. A cup of it has half of your vitamin C requirement for the day. It's also a good source of dietary fiber, potassium, and vitamin B. The produce associate at our grocery store said that the best way to detect a ripe honeydew melon is to push gently against the skin. The melon should be slightly soft—if it is firm, it is not ripe yet.

TROPICAL GREEN SMOOTHIE

HAVE YOU EVER ADDED OATS TO A SMOOTHIE? OATS THICKEN THE MIXTURE, AND THE WHOLE GRAINS ADD NUTRITION. YOU COULD EVEN MAKE THIS SMOOTHIE A MEAL BY ADDING A HANDFUL OF NUTS AS A SIDE DISH. IT IS A GREAT START TO YOUR DAY!

INGREDIENTS

1 cup coconut milk or almond milk

1 handful of spinach

1/4 cup old-fashioned oats

1 tablespoon chia seeds

1 tablespoon flaxseed

1/2 cup fresh or frozen mango chunks

1/4 cup fresh or frozen pineapple chunks

1 banana, chopped and frozen

Honey to taste (optional)

SERVES 1–2

1 Pour all ingredients into a blender in the order listed and let them whirl until combined. For additional sweetness, add a little honey. If you want the smoothie to have a thinner consistency, increase the liquid.

2 Enjoy immediately.

TIP:

If your blender has less-than-stellar performance, add the oats first and blend into a powder. Then remove the oat powder, add the other smoothie ingredients, and pour the oat powder back in to finish blending.

CHIA FRESCA

MY SISTER THINKS IT'S FUN TO BUY CHIA DRINKS FROM THE STORE. BUT WE ENJOY MAKING OUR OWN, WHICH GIVES US THE ABILITY TO CONTROL WHAT IS IN THEM. HERE IS A QUICK AND EASY RECIPE THAT TASTES GREAT. ENJOYING THIS DRINK IS A WONDERFUL WAY TO BOOST YOUR ENERGY FOR THE DAY.

1 Pour all ingredients into a quart jar, cover with a lid, and shake until mixed.

2 Leave in the refrigerator for at least 30 minutes to let the chia soften and expand. It's a great drink to enjoy all day long.

INGREDIENTS

1 cup pure, unsweetened pomegranate cranberry juice

3 cups water

3 tablespoons chia seeds

3–4 tablespoons honey

Juice from 1 lime

SERVES 1–2

TIP:

Vary the type of juice you use to change the flavor of this recipe. Be sure to include only unsweetened juice in order to avoid consuming too much sugar.

ALMOND JOY® SMOOTHIE

HERE IS A FUN WAY TO ENJOY THE FLAVORS OF AN ALMOND JOY® WITHOUT FEELING ANY GUILT. IT'S A CANDY BAR IN A GLASS! WE ADDED A BANANA FOR NATURAL SWEETNESS INSTEAD OF ADDING SUGAR. YOU CAN BLEND IT AS SMOOTH AS YOU WANT IF YOU DON'T WANT THE SMOOTHIE TO HAVE A DISTINCT TEXTURE. HOWEVER, I ENJOYED A LITTLE TEXTURE IN MINE.

INGREDIENTS

2 cups unsweetened vanilla almond milk

1/2 cup unsweetened shredded coconut

1/4 cup dark chocolate chips (70 percent cocoa or greater)

1/4 cup almonds

2 tablespoons chia seeds

1 banana, chopped and frozen

Extra unsweetened shredded coconut and crushed dark chocolate chips for toppings (optional)

SERVES 2

1 Pour all ingredients except the toppings into a blender in the order listed. Blend to desired texture.

2 Garnish with coconut and crushed chocolate chips, if desired.

CHOCOLATE PEANUT BUTTER CUP DREAM

WE CAN'T GET ENOUGH OF PEANUT BUTTER AND CHOCOLATE COMBINED. THIS SMOOTHIE HAS ALL THE RIGHT FLAVORS WITHOUT SACRIFICING NUTRITION. IT IS GOOD TO THE LAST DROP, WITH NO ADDED SUGAR.

1   Pour the milk, cocoa, bananas, chia, and peanut butter into a blender. Blend the mixture until creamy.

2   Add the chocolate chips and ice. Blend mixture again until creamy.

3   Garnish with chopped chocolate chips, if desired, and serve immediately.

INGREDIENTS

2 cups cashew milk (or milk of your choosing)

1 tablespoon cocoa powder

2 bananas, frozen

2 tablespoons chia seeds

3 tablespoons natural creamy peanut butter

1/4 cup dark chocolate chips (70 percent cocoa or greater)

8 ice cubes

Chopped dark chocolate chips for topping (optional)

SERVES 2

BREADS

PUMPKIN SPICE MUFFINS

PUMPKIN MUFFINS ARE MOM'S ABSOLUTE FAVORITE KIND OF MUFFINS, AND THESE FIT THE BILL NICELY. THEY ARE MOIST AND HAVE FANTASTIC FLAVOR. I LOVED ADDING THE CHIA FOR EXTRA PROTEIN.

INGREDIENTS

1 cup buttermilk

1/2 cup honey

2 tablespoons coconut oil

2 eggs

1/3 cup chia seeds

1 teaspoon vanilla

1 1/4 cups 100 percent pure canned pumpkin puree

3/4 teaspoon pumpkin pie spice

1/2 teaspoon salt

1 tablespoon baking powder

2 cups spelt flour or another whole grain flour

MAKES 30 MINI MUFFINS

1 Preheat oven to 375 degrees. In a blender, beat together the buttermilk, honey, oil, eggs, and chia and then pulse in the vanilla. Next, pulse in the pumpkin puree. Set the mixture aside for 5–10 minutes.

2 In a separate medium bowl, combine the pumpkin spice, salt, baking powder, and flour. Stir them together with a wire whisk.

3 Take the blender mixture and fold into the mixture in the bowl. Stir until combined.

4 Grease a mini muffin pan and scoop the batter into it.

5 Place the pan in the heated oven. Bake muffins for 10–12 minutes or until a toothpick inserted in the center comes out clean.

6 Remove from the oven and cool on a wire rack for 5 minutes, then remove the muffins from the pan.

TIP:

We often make mini muffins, but you can adjust these recipes for any size of muffin. To make standard-sized muffins, add 5–8 minutes of baking time. Add 15–20 minutes to make jumbo muffins. There are about 3 mini muffins in a standard muffin.

TIP:
If you get in a bind and don't have buttermilk, pour 1 tablespoon of vinegar in a 1-cup measuring cup then fill up the rest of the cup with milk. Let it sit for 20 minutes. It will curdle, so you can use it in place of buttermilk.

ORANGE BRAN MUFFINS

MY MOM'S MUFFINS ARE THE ONE THING THAT MY PICKY SONS WILL ALWAYS EAT, AND THEY LOVE THESE MUFFINS IN PARTICULAR. BRAN WITH AN ORANGE TWIST IS A GREAT COMBINATION. WE LIKE EATING THEM HOT OUT OF THE OVEN.

INGREDIENTS

1/3 cup bran

1/2 cup raisins

1 cup unsweetened almond milk

Freshly squeezed juice from 2 oranges

1/3 cup chia seeds

2 tablespoons orange zest

2 eggs

2 tablespoons coconut oil

1/2 cup honey

2 cups spelt flour or another whole grain flour

2 teaspoons baking powder

1/2 teaspoon salt

1 cup unsweetened shredded coconut

MAKES 12 MUFFINS

1 Preheat oven to 350 degrees. Pour the bran into a mixing bowl. Then pour in the raisins, milk, juice, and chia. Stir until all ingredients are moistened. Set mixture aside for about 10 minutes to let the bran soften.

2 After the bran has softened, add the orange zest, eggs, oil, and honey to the mixture. Stir until all ingredients are combined.

3 In a separate medium bowl, stir together the flour, baking powder, and salt. Then add the bran mixture, stirring until just combined. Finally, stir in the coconut.

4 Scoop the muffin batter into a greased muffin tin.

5 Place the tin in the heated oven. Bake muffins for 10–12 minutes or until a toothpick inserted in the center comes out clean.

6 Remove from oven and cool muffins on a wire rack for about 5 minutes, then remove the muffins from the pan.

TIP:

Here are some suggestions for other fun add-ins that will personalize your muffins.

- 1/2 cup mini dark chocolate chips (70 percent cocoa or greater)
- 1/2 cup chopped apples
- 1/2 cup dried fruit

CHOCOLATE CHIP CHUNKY BARS

THINK OF THESE AS HEALTHY COOKIES IN BAR FORM, BUT THEY ARE SO MUCH FASTER TO MAKE! THESE ARE HEALTHY ENOUGH IN OUR BOOK TO ENJOY FOR A SWEET BREAKFAST OR AN AFTER-SCHOOL SNACK.

1 In a bowl, beat together the oil and honey. Then beat in each egg, one at a time. Finally, stir in the chia and vanilla.

2 In a separate large bowl, stir together the oats, flour, baking soda, and salt.

3 Combine the wet and dry mixtures, stirring until just mixed. Fold in the chocolate chips.

4 Scoop batter into a 9 x 9–inch pan. Spread until batter is smooth and evenly distributed.

5 Place pan in the heated oven and bake for 25–30 minutes or until a toothpick inserted in the center comes out clean.

6 Remove from oven, cool, and then cut into squares.

INGREDIENTS

3/4 cup coconut oil

3/4 cup honey

2 eggs

1/3 cup chia seeds

1 teaspoon vanilla

2 cups old-fashioned oats

1 cup whole grain flour (we used Kamut®)

3/4 teaspoon baking soda

1/4 teaspoon salt

1 cup dark chocolate chips (70 percent cocoa or greater)

SERVES 9

DID YOU KNOW?

Historically, chia has been used medicinally as a poultice for wounds. The wound was packed with chia because it was believed to help avoid infection of the injury and promote healing.

WHOLE GRAIN OAT BREAD

THE TASTE OF THIS BREAD REMINDS US OF THE KIND THAT WE LOVE AT RESTAURANTS—
SPECKLED WITH OATS ON THE SIDES. IT WAS FUN TO CREATE A WHOLE-GRAIN BREAD THAT
HAS THE SAME FLAVOR.

INGREDIENTS

1 1/2 cups old-fashioned oats

2 tablespoons butter or coconut oil

1 1/2 cup boiling water

1/3 cup honey

1/4 cup chia seeds

1 tablespoon salt

1 1/2 cups warm water (about 110 degrees)

3 1/2 teaspoons yeast

6 1/2–7 cups whole grain flour

1 1/2 cup rolled oats

MAKES TWO
9-INCH LOAVES

1 In a metal bowl, combine the oats and butter or coconut oil. Then pour the boiling water over both. Stir until all ingredients are mixed. Set the mixture aside and let it cool to room temperature. You could start the soaking process the night before and let it sit overnight to increase the nutritional benefits.

2 Pour all other ingredients except the rolled oats into a bread mixer. Add 1 cup of flour at a time until the dough pulls away from the sides of the bowl. Don't let it get too dry; the dough should still be sticky.

3 Let the mixer knead the dough for 3–4 minutes. Let the dough rest for 10 minutes. Then turn on the mixer and let it knead for 2 more minutes.

4 Place the dough in a slightly oiled bowl that is twice the size of the dough. Cover the bowl with plastic wrap and let the dough rise until it has doubled. Then deflate the dough, cover the bowl with plastic wrap, and let the dough double one more time.

5 Punch down the dough. Divide the dough in half and roll each half into a loaf.

6 Pour 3/4 cup of the rolled oats onto a rectangular piece of parchment paper. Spread the oats in a rectangle and roll the first loaf in the oats until the top and sides of the loaf are covered. Discard the leftover oats and repeat the

process with the remaining 3/4 cup of rolled oats for the second loaf.

7 Place each loaf in a 9-inch greased bread pan. Cover the pans with plastic wrap. Again, let the dough double until the loaves are 1 inch above the rim of the bread pans.

8 Preheat oven to 400 degrees.

9 Bake each loaf for about 45 minutes or until the internal temperature is 200 degrees and the outside is golden brown.

10 Rub the bread with butter if desired—the butter keeps the crust soft. Place the bread on its side, to keep the loaf from falling, on a wire rack to cool—if it lasts that long. We love to eat it when it is warm.

TIP:

For the whole grain flour, we used a mixture of 3 1/2 cups whole wheat flour and 3 1/2 cups spelt flour.

CHOCOLATE PUMPKIN BREAD

USING MASHED BANANAS IN QUICK BREAD RECIPES ADDS A NATURAL SWEETNESS TO THE BREAD WITHOUT ADDING EXTRA SUGAR OR FAT. THIS BREAD IS MOIST AND TASTES SO GOOD. YOU COULD ALSO USE THIS RECIPE TO MAKE MUFFINS.

1 Preheat oven to 350 degrees. Grease a 13 x 9–inch pan.

2 Mix together the dry ingredients in a large bowl. In another bowl, combine the pumpkin puree, oil, eggs, water, milk, syrup, and bananas.

3 Add the wet ingredients to the dry ingredients and stir until just combined. Pour mixture into a greased pan.

4 Place pan in the heated oven. Bake for 30 minutes or until a toothpick inserted in the center comes out clean.

SERVES 12

TIP:

When baking with whole grains, we have found that stoneware pans yield better results. Be it bread, muffins, cake, or bars, they bake more evenly on stoneware.

INGREDIENTS

3 1/2 cups spelt flour or another whole grain flour

1/2 cup chia seeds

2 teaspoons baking soda

1 teaspoon baking powder

3/4 teaspoon salt

2 teaspoons nutmeg

2 teaspoons cinnamon

1/4 cup cocoa

1 can (15 ounces) 100 percent pure pumpkin puree or 2 cups fresh pumpkin puree

1/2 cup olive oil

2 eggs

1/2 cup water

1 cup unsweetened vanilla almond milk

1 cup maple syrup

1 cup mashed bananas

CHOCOLATE CHIP MUFFINS

THIS IS A SUPER EASY WHOLE GRAIN RECIPE. I CHOPPED UP THE CHOCOLATE CHIPS, WHICH ADDED A LITTLE BIT OF CHOCOLATE TO EVERY BITE. THESE MUFFINS MAKE A GREAT SNACK OR A NICE ADDITION TO A MEAL.

INGREDIENTS

2/3 cup honey

1/2 cup olive oil or coconut oil

1/2 cup almond milk

1/2 cup water

2 eggs

1/4 teaspoon salt

1/4 cup chia seeds

1 1/2 teaspoons baking powder

1 cup whole wheat flour

1/2 cup chopped dark chocolate chips (70 percent cocoa or greater)

MAKES 12 MINI MUFFINS

1 Preheat oven to 400 degrees. Beat or stir together the honey, oil, milk, and water. Beat or stir in the eggs. Set mixture aside.

2 In a separate large bowl, mix together the salt, chia, baking powder, and flour.

3 Fold the wet mixture into the dry mixture and stir until just combined. Fold in the chocolate chips.

4 Grease a muffin tin. Scoop the muffin mix into the tin.

5 Place tin in the oven and bake for 12–15 minutes or until a toothpick inserted in the center comes out clean.

6 Let the muffins sit in the tin for 5 minutes and then remove. Cool the muffins on a wire rack before enjoying.

DID YOU KNOW?

Why use honey instead of sugar? Honey isn't a mixture of fructose or glucose but a mixture of compounds and minerals. It doesn't spike your blood sugar as much as other types of sugars, nor does it cause as much inflammation in your body.

BERRY BERRY MUFFINS

WE LOVE BERRIES! MY KIDS AND I GOBBLED THESE MUFFINS UP, WHICH IS ALWAYS A GOOD SIGN.

1 Preheat oven to 350 degrees. Beat together the oil, honey, water, and milk. Then beat in the eggs, one at a time.

2 In another bowl, mix together the chia, baking powder, and flour. Fold the wet batter into the dry ingredients and mix until just combined. Gently fold in the berries.

3 Scoop batter into a greased muffin tin and place in the heated oven. Bake for 15–20 minutes or until done.

4 Take the muffin tin out of the oven and let sit for 5 minutes before removing the muffins to cool on a wire rack.

INGREDIENTS

1/2 cup coconut oil

1/2 cup honey

1/2 cup water

1/2 cup almond milk or cashew milk

2 eggs

1/4 cup chia seeds

2 teaspoons baking powder

2 cups whole wheat flour

1 cup mixed berries (blueberries, raspberries, and strawberries), chopped

MAKES 12 MUFFINS

SNACKS

CHERRY CHOCOLATE CARAMEL GRANOLA BARS

THIS IS A HEALTHY SNACK THAT IS FULL OF PROTEIN AND ANTIOXIDANTS AND IS LOW IN SUGAR. MY SISTER SAYS SHE DOESN'T LIKE CHERRIES, BUT SHE REALLY LIKED THESE. SHE EVEN PACKED SOME FOR WORK. THESE ARE ALSO HEALTHY ENOUGH TO EAT FOR BREAKFAST.

INGREDIENTS

1 cup canned coconut milk (full fat)

1/4 cup honey

2 tablespoons coconut oil

1/2 cup chia seeds

1/2 cup unsweetened shredded coconut

2 cups old-fashioned oats

1/2 cup dried cherries, diced

1/2 cup dark chocolate chips (70 percent cocoa or greater), chopped

1 Grease a 9 x 9–inch pan or line it with parchment paper. Set the pan aside.

2 Pour the milk, honey, and oil into a small saucepan. Stir the mixture on medium to medium-low heat, being careful not to let it burn. Let it cook, stirring often, until it becomes thick like caramel—or is at soft-ball stage.

3 In a medium bowl, combine the chia, coconut, oats, and cherries. Stir together until all ingredients are combined.

4 Pour the hot caramel over the oat mixture. Stir until all ingredients are completely mixed together. Fold in the chocolate chips.

5 Pour mixture into the lined or greased pan. Press the mixture down with a spatula.

6 Place in the refrigerator to harden for at least half an hour. When the mixture has hardened, cut it into 16 squares. Store bars in an airtight container in the refrigerator.

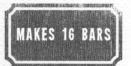

MAKES 16 BARS

CHEWY PROTEIN ENERGY BARS

THESE ENERGY BARS ARE LOADED WITH PROTEIN, ARE LOW IN SUGAR, AND TASTE GREAT. YOU CAN MAKE THEM YOUR OWN BY BEING CREATIVE AND ADDING YOUR FAVORITE DRIED FRUIT, OR YOU CAN LEAVE THE RECIPE AS IT IS. I LOVED THE SOFT CHEWINESS OF THESE BARS.

INGREDIENTS

1/2 cup chia seeds, ground

1 cup old-fashioned oats

1/2 cup sunflower seeds

1/4 cup spelt or another whole grain flour

1/2 cup dried fruit of your choosing (optional)

1/2 cup raw almonds

1/2 cup raisins

1/2 cup soft dates

1 teaspoon cinnamon

2 tablespoons coconut oil

5 tablespoons honey

2 eggs

MAKES 9 BARS

1 Preheat oven to 350 degrees. In a blender or food processor, pulse and blend everything except the oil, honey, and eggs until broken down.

2 Pour the mixture into a large bowl and add the oil, honey, and eggs. Using a wire whisk, whip until all ingredients are combined. The mixture should be a thick paste.

3 Grease a 9 x 9–inch pan or line it with parchment paper. Press the mixture into the pan.

4 Place pan in the heated oven and bake for 15 minutes.

5 Take the pan out of the oven and let cool, about 15 minutes, before cutting and removing the bars from the pan.

6 Wrap the bars individually with plastic wrap and store in an airtight container so they are ready to grab when you need a healthy snack. You can store them in the refrigerator for 3 days or freeze them for up to 3 months.

TIP:

It is easy to find many energy bars in the store, but they are usually expensive and you often need a dictionary to decipher the ingredients. The safest and healthiest bet is to make your own. The key is to make a batch of them ahead of time so that they are ready to go when you need them.

PEANUT BUTTER NUT CLUSTERS

WE LOVE THESE CLUSTERS! THEY ARE LOADED WITH PROTEIN AND MAKE A GREAT SNACK IN BETWEEN MEALS. THEY ARE DELICIOUS AND HEALTHY NO-BAKE COOKIES.

1 Line a cookie sheet with parchment paper. Put all ingredients in a blender or food processor and pulse until combined.

2 Roll the batter into 1-inch balls and place on the cookie sheet.

3 Place clusters in the refrigerator to harden. Enjoy immediately or store in an airtight container in the refrigerator.

INGREDIENTS

1/4 cup pecans

1/4 cup almonds

1/2 cup cashews

1/4 cup natural creamy peanut butter

1/4 cup chia seeds

1 tablespoon coconut oil

3/4 cup old-fashioned oats

1/3 cup dark chocolate chips (70 percent cocoa or greater)

MAKES 12 CLUSTERS

PUMPKIN CHOCOLATE CHIP BITES

THESE ARE FUN LITTLE SNACKS, AND THEY ARE LOADED WITH PROTEIN. OUR GOAL IS TO CUT DOWN ON SUGAR IN THESE RECIPES WITHOUT SACRIFICING FLAVOR. THESE BITES DO JUST THAT! THEY ARE GREAT TO MAKE AHEAD OF TIME AND HAVE IN THE REFRIGERATOR FOR WHEN YOU WANT A HEALTHY SNACK.

INGREDIENTS

1 cup of dates that have been soaked in water for at least an hour

2 tablespoons coconut oil

1/2 cup 100 percent pure canned pumpkin puree

1/2 cup old-fashioned oats

1/2 cup cashews, chopped

4 tablespoons chia seeds

1/2 cup dark chocolate chips (70 percent cocoa or greater)

MAKES 12 BITES

1 Blend the dates and oil together in a blender or food processor until smooth.

2 Add in the pumpkin puree and blend again until smooth.

3 Add the oats, cashews, chia, and chocolate chips and blend until all ingredients are combined and the chocolate chips are broken down. You may have to stop and stir the mixture several times because it is so thick.

4 Put the mixture in a bowl in the refrigerator for 20 minutes to make it easier to handle.

5 Form the mixture into balls and put them back in the refrigerator in an airtight container. Eat the bites after they've hardened a bit. Store the leftovers in the airtight container.

CHUNKY MONKEY BARS

THESE NO-BAKE BARS NOT ONLY HAVE THE PERFECT COMBINATION OF PEANUT BUTTER AND CHOCOLATE, BUT THEY ARE ALSO FAST AND EASY TO MAKE.

1 Combine all ingredients in a medium bowl and stir.

2 Grease a 9-inch loaf pan. Press the mixture into the pan and put in the refrigerator to harden for at least an hour.

3 Cut the hardened mixture into 10 squares. Store leftovers in an airtight container in the refrigerator.

INGREDIENTS

2 cups old-fashioned oats

1 cup natural creamy peanut butter

1–2 tablespoons honey (substitute date paste for a vegan version)

2 tablespoons coconut oil

1 tablespoon cocoa powder

2 tablespoons chia seeds

MAKES 10 BARS

CHOCOLATE CASHEW PROTEIN BITES

WHEN IT'S TIME FOR A SNACK, IT IS SO EASY TO REACH FOR THE FIRST THING THAT IS AVAILABLE, BE IT HEALTHY OR NOT. THAT IS WHY WE MAKE SO MANY VARIETIES OF THESE BITES. IT'S GREAT TO HAVE HEALTHY, FILLING TREATS LIKE THESE ON HAND WHEN YOU NEED A SNACK.

INGREDIENTS

- 1 cup cashews
- 2 tablespoons chia seeds
- 2 tablespoons hemp seeds
- 2 tablespoons coconut oil
- 1 tablespoon cocoa powder
- 1 tablespoon honey

MAKES 5–6 BITES

1 Pulse the cashews in a blender or food processor, leaving them a little chunky.

2 Add the remaining ingredients into the blender or food processor. Pulse until all ingredients are combined. You may have to stir the mixture with a rubber spatula in between pulses if the thick batter pushes to the sides of the blender or food processor.

3 Pour the mixture into a bowl and form into balls. Put the balls in the refrigerator to harden for at least half an hour.

4 Store the bites in an airtight container in the refrigerator and enjoy them as desired.

DID YOU KNOW?

You can find and purchase chia in several different forms—whole chia seeds, chia bran, ground chia, and chia seed oil. However, whole seeds have the longest shelf life and are the best choice for long-term storage.

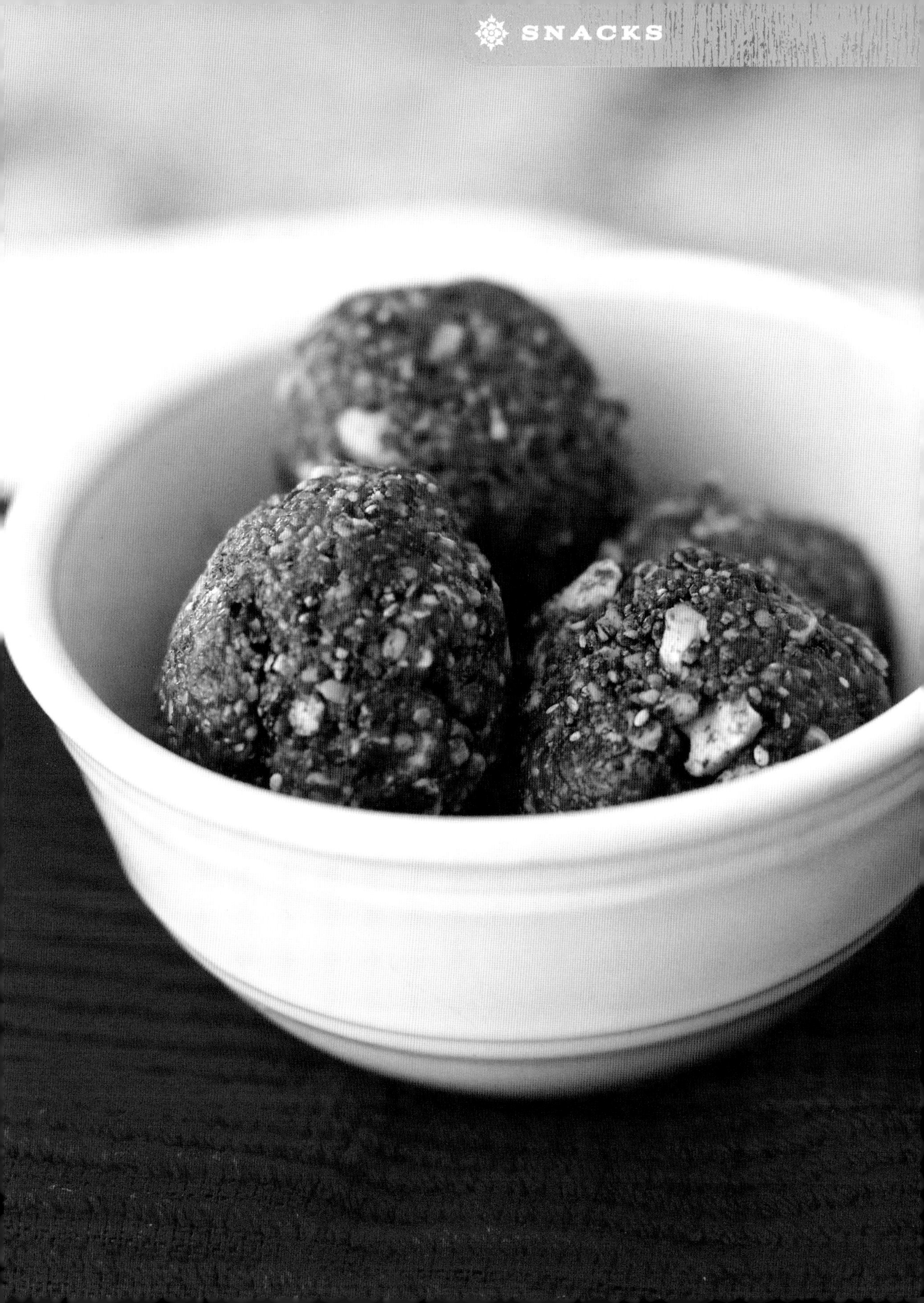

CHOCOLATE PEANUT BUTTER DOUGH BITES

DO YOU EVER CRAVE COOKIE DOUGH? WE SURE DO. THIS IS A GREAT WAY TO SATISFY THAT CRAVING WITHOUT ALL THE CALORIES. YOU CAN MAKE THESE BITES AHEAD OF TIME SO THAT YOU HAVE THEM READY WHEN YOUR SWEET SNACK CRAVING HITS. THEY ARE ALSO HIGH IN PROTEIN, SO ENJOY THEM GUILT-FREE!

INGREDIENTS

1/3 cup natural creamy peanut butter

1/4 cup honey

3 tablespoons coconut oil

1 teaspoon vanilla

1 cup old-fashioned oats

3/4 cup unsweetened shredded coconut

1/3 cup dark chocolate chips (70 percent cocoa or greater), chopped

1/3 cup chia seeds, ground

1 In a mixing bowl, combine the peanut butter, honey, oil, and vanilla. Stir together until completely mixed and creamy.

2 Add the rest of the ingredients into the bowl. Stir until combined. Use your clean hands to help combine the ingredients, if necessary.

3 Roll scoops of batter into 1-inch balls with your hands. Place on a non-stick surface or a cookie sheet lined with parchment paper.

4 Put bites in the refrigerator to harden for at least half an hour. After the bites harden, enjoy them or store them in an airtight container in the refrigerator or freezer.

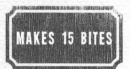

MAKES 15 BITES

APPLE SANDWICHES

WE LOVE THIS IDEA OF USING APPLES INSTEAD OF BREAD FOR A CHANGE. YOU CAN GET AS CREATIVE AS YOU WANT AND ADD FUN TOPPINGS TO THE SANDWICHES. THEY ARE A DELICIOUS SNACK!

1 Cut thin, round slices off the apple on one side until you get to the core. Then slice the other side of the apple.

2 Spread the peanut butter on half of the apple slices, sprinkle on the chia, and then top with raisins or chocolate chips. Top with the other apple slices.

3 Serve immediately.

INGREDIENTS

1 apple

3 tablespoons natural creamy peanut butter (or any kind of nut butter)

1 1/2 teaspoon chia seeds

Raisins or dark chocolate chips (70 percent cocoa or greater) for topping

MAKES 3 SANDWICHES

RAW GRANOLA

THIS IS A FAST AND EASY WAY TO MAKE GRANOLA—NO BAKING IS REQUIRED. IT TASTES LIKE YOU ARE EATING OATMEAL CHOCOLATE CHIP COOKIE DOUGH, AND IT MAKES A GREAT SNACK OR A FUN BREAKFAST.

1 Combine all ingredients except the chocolate chips in a bowl. Mix until combined.

2 Add the chocolate chips and stir until just combined. Eat granola immediately or store in an airtight container in the refrigerator to enjoy later.

INGREDIENTS

1/2 cup honey

1/2 cup coconut oil, melted

1/2 teaspoon salt

1 cup unsweetened coconut flakes

1 cup almonds, chopped

1/2 cup chia seeds

4 cups old-fashioned oats

1/2 teaspoon almond extract (optional)

1/2 cup dark chocolate chips (70 percent cocoa or greater), chopped

MAKES ABOUT 5 CUPS

DID YOU KNOW?

One recent study found that chia may benefit athletes. Results showed that athletes who drank a 50:50 caloric mix of Gatorade® and chia performed just as well as those who drank pure Gatorade®. Try adding chia to your sports drinks!

FRUIT-AND-NUT CHOCOLATE BITES

THESE ARE INSPIRED BY THE CHOCOLATE CHERRY KIND® BARS. THEY ARE SO EXPENSIVE TO PURCHASE, SO I THOUGHT IT WOULD BE FUN TO MAKE MY OWN HEALTHY VERSION OF THEM. THERE IS NO ADDED SUGAR IN THIS LITTLE SNACK.

INGREDIENTS

3/4 cup dark chocolate chips (70 percent cocoa or greater) for melting

1 tablespoon coconut oil

1 cup dried fruit (we used 1/2 cup cherries and 1/2 cup pomegranates)

2 tablespoons coconut oil

5 tablespoons chia seeds

1 cup unsalted cashews

1 cup unsalted almonds

1/4 cup dark chocolate chips (70 percent cocoa or greater)

MAKES ABOUT 12 BITES

1 In a small bowl, combine the chocolate chips and oil. Heat in a microwave for 1 minute and then stir. Heat the mixture again for 1 minute. Stir again and place in the refrigerator to thicken a little.

2 Combine the rest of the ingredients (including the remaining 1/4 cup of chocolate chips) in a blender or food processor. Pulse and stir until mixed, leaving the nuts a little chunky.

3 Scoop and roll mixture into 1-inch balls. Prepare a greased or non-stick surface.

4 Take the melted chocolate out of the refrigerator. Dip the balls into the chocolate and place onto the greased or non-stick surface.

5 Place bites in the refrigerator to harden for at least a half an hour. Store in an airtight container in the refrigerator and eat as desired.

SOUPS

MULLIGATAWNY SOUP

THIS RICH CURRIED SOUP IS BASED ON A SAUCE FROM INDIA THAT WAS POPULAR WITH MEMBERS OF THE EAST INDIA TRADING COMPANY STATIONED THERE AT THE BEGINNING OF THE CENTURY. THEY BROUGHT THEIR OWN VARIATIONS OF IT BACK HOME TO BRITAIN AND AUSTRALIA. HERE IS A HEALTHY VERSION WE MADE.

INGREDIENTS

3 tablespoons olive oil

1 large onion, chopped

3 carrots, chopped

4 stalks celery, chopped

1 large tart apple (like Granny Smith), peeled, cored, and chopped

2 tablespoons whole grain flour

1/4 cup chia seeds

2 teaspoons curry powder

1 1/2 teaspoons salt

1/2 teaspoon thyme

5 1/2 cups water

1 can (14.5 ounces) whole tomatoes

2 cups cooked brown rice

Plain yogurt for garnish (optional)

1 Heat the oil in large pot on medium. Add the onion, carrots, celery, and apple. Stir until soft and slightly browned.

2 Stir in the flour and continue stirring for 1 minute until the flour is completely integrated. Then stir in the chia, curry powder, salt, and thyme.

3 Add the water and bring the soup to a boil. Then stir in the tomatoes. Turn down the heat and put the lid on the pot. Let the soup simmer on low for about 30 minutes.

4 Pour the soup into a blender or food processor and pulse until smooth.

5 Return the soup to the pot and stir in the rice. Heat the soup until the rice is warm.

6 Serve hot. Top with a dollop of plain yogurt, if desired.

SERVES 4

LENTIL CHICKEN STEW

THIS STEW IS A DELICIOUS BLEND OF VEGETABLES, LEGUMES, AND FRESH CHICKEN, AND WE FIND IT IS VERY FILLING. THE SWEET POTATO IS A FANTASTIC SWEETENING TOUCH, AND THE CHIA HELPS MAKE THE SOUP EVEN MORE FILLING, WHICH IS GREAT IF YOU'RE TRYING TO CUT DOWN ON CALORIES.

INGREDIENTS

3 tablespoons olive oil

1 onion, chopped

2 cloves garlic, minced

1 pound diced chicken breast

1 teaspoon marjoram

1 teaspoon thyme

2 teaspoons salt

1/2 teaspoon pepper

1/8 teaspoon ground allspice (optional)

1/2 cup chia seeds, ground

1 can (14 ounces) diced tomatoes

6 cups water

1 cup lentils, dried

4 stalks celery, chopped

1 sweet potato, chopped

1 Heat the oil in a large pot on medium heat and toss in the onion and garlic. Stir and sauté for about 5 minutes until soft.

2 Stir in the diced chicken and cook all the way through.

3 Stir in the rest of the ingredients and bring to a boil. Turn the heat down to medium low. Cook the soup 30–45 minutes or until the potatoes and lentils are soft.

4 Serve the soup in bowls. You can store leftovers in an airtight container in the refrigerator or freezer.

SERVES 8

VEGETABLE BEAN SOUP

THIS SOUP IS LOADED WITH VEGETABLES AND LOTS OF FLAVOR. WE FIND IT IS A GREAT WAY TO WARM UP ON COLD DAYS.

1 Warm the oil in a large cooking pot on medium heat.

2 When the oil is hot, add the onion and garlic and sauté until soft and light golden.

3 Add the chili, chicken, and water. Cook the chicken until it is mostly cooked.

4 Stir in the celery, carrots, water, thyme, salt, pepper, oregano, and chia. Let the mixture come to a boil, then turn down the heat and let simmer for 20 minutes or until the vegetables start to soften.

5 Puree the tomatoes in a blender and then add them to the soup. Stir in the beans and let simmer for another 20 minutes.

6 Remove the soup from heat and serve in soup bowls with desired toppings. Store leftovers in an airtight container in the refrigerator or freezer.

INGREDIENTS

3 tablespoons olive oil

1 onion, diced

3 cloves garlic, minced

1/4 red chili, finely chopped and deseeded

1 boneless, skinless chicken breast, chopped

1/4 cup water

4 stalks celery, chopped

1 cup chopped carrots

6 cups water

1/2 teaspoon thyme

1 teaspoon salt

1/4 teaspoon pepper

1/2 teaspoon oregano

1/3 cup chia seeds

1 can (14.5 ounces) whole tomatoes

1 can (14 ounces) great northern beans, drained and rinsed

Cilantro, parsley, cheese, or tortilla chips for toppings

TIP:

This recipe calls for great northern beans, but you can change them out for a different type, if you prefer. Garbanzo or black beans would also be delicious in this soup.

SERVES 6

WHITE CHICKEN CHILI

THIS IS ONE OF MY FAMILY'S FAVORITE DINNERS. IT IS A WONDERFUL, HEARTY CHILI FULL OF VEGETABLES. IT COOKS UP FAST AND IS GREAT FOR EITHER A SMALL GROUP OR A BIG GATHERING.

INGREDIENTS

3–4 tablespoons olive oil

2 cups chopped chicken (you could also use turkey)

1 cup chopped onions

1 red pepper, deseeded and diced

3 cloves garlic, minced

1/2 cup chia seeds

4 cups water

2 teaspoons salt

1 teaspoon cumin

1 can (4 ounces) diced green chilies

1 can (11 ounces) white shoepeg corn

Juice from 2 limes

2 cans (14 ounces each) great northern beans, drained and rinsed

Tortilla chips and grated Monterey Jack cheese for toppings (optional)

1 In a large pot, heat the oil on medium heat. Add the chicken and cook until lightly browned.

2 Add the onions, pepper, garlic, and chia. Continue to cook the mixture on medium heat. You may need to add a little more oil. Cook until the vegetables are soft and slightly browned. (The browning adds extra flavor.)

3 Stir in the water, salt, cumin, chilies, corn, and lime juice. Let the mixture come to a boil.

4 Turn the heat to low and stir in the beans. Cover and let simmer for 30–40 minutes.

5 Serve in bowls and top with chips and cheese, if desired. Store leftovers in an airtight container in the refrigerator.

DID YOU KNOW?

Just one ounce—about two tablespoons—of chia contains four grams of protein, nine grams of healthy fats, eleven grams of fiber, and additional vitamins and minerals—talk about nutrient packed!

SERVES 6

INDIAN SPICED CAULIFLOWER SOUP

THIS IS A FUN WAY TO USE CAULIFLOWER, AND ADDING SOME INDIAN SPICES TO THE SOUP MAKES IT A DELICIOUS LUNCH OR DINNER. MY ONE-YEAR-OLD KEPT ASKING FOR SECONDS, THIRDS, AND EVEN FOURTHS OF THIS SOUP BECAUSE IT'S SO GOOD!

INGREDIENTS

1 large head of cauliflower, chopped

6–7 tablespoons olive oil

1 cup chopped carrots

1 onion, chopped

3 cloves garlic, minced

2 teaspoons grated ginger root

1/4 cup chia seeds

1 teaspoon cumin

1 teaspoon black mustard seeds

2 teaspoons turmeric

1 teaspoon salt

4 1/2 cups water

1/2 cup plain yogurt

Naan flatbread (optional)

SERVES 4

1 Preheat oven to 375 degrees. Place cauliflower on a cookie sheet and drizzle with 3–4 tablespoons of the olive oil. Place the cookie sheet on the middle rack of the oven and roast for 25–30 minutes or until the cauliflower starts to soften.

2 Pour the remaining 3 tablespoons of oil into a large soup pot and add the roasted cauliflower, carrots, onion, garlic, ginger, chia, cumin, mustard seeds, turmeric, and salt. Sauté together on medium heat for 5–10 minutes or until the vegetables start to soften.

3 Stir in the water and let the mixture come to a low boil. Turn the heat down to medium low and put the lid on the pot. Cook the soup for 30 minutes, stirring occasionally.

4 Put the warm soup mixture into a blender and puree. You may have to do it in two batches, depending on the size of your blender. Then blend in the yogurt.

5 Serve warm with naan flatbread, if desired.

TURKEY QUINOA SOUP

THE HOUSE SMELLS SO GOOD WHILE THIS HEARTY SOUP IS COOKING ON THE STOVE. SOUP OUT OF A CAN JUST DOESN'T GIVE OFF THE SAME MOUTHWATERING AROMA. IF YOU DON'T HAVE A TURKEY CARCASS, YOU CAN MAKE THE SOUP WITH CHOPPED TURKEY INSTEAD. THE CHIA NICELY THICKENS THE SOUP.

1 If you are using a turkey carcass, place the carcass in a large stockpot and cover it with water. Heat on low and cook for about 3 hours or until the meat starts to fall off the bones. Take the pot off the stove and strain the mixture to remove the fat and bones. Leave the broth and meat in the stockpot and place it back on the stove. Add water to make a total of 8 cups of liquid.

2 If you don't have a turkey carcass, simmer the chopped turkey in 8 cups of water for 20 minutes. This will become your broth.

3 Add the remaining ingredients and simmer for at least another 30 minutes to soften the vegetables and cook the quinoa. Add more water if the soup gets too thick.

4 Serve in soup bowls.

INGREDIENTS

1 turkey carcass or 4 cups of cooked and chopped turkey

8 cups water

1 cup quinoa, well rinsed

3/4 cup chia seeds

1 cup chopped carrots

1 cup chopped celery

1 onion, chopped

3 cloves garlic, minced

1 teaspoon salt

1 teaspoon marjoram

1 teaspoon thyme

1/2 teaspoon rosemary

1/4 teaspoon pepper

Additional salt and pepper to taste (optional)

SERVES 8

DID YOU KNOW?

Quinoa (pronounced *keen-wa*) is a superfood that contains more protein than any other grain. It is also a complete protein and is high in lysine. It can be used as a more nutritious substitute for rice.

SALADS & SIDES

COWBOY CAVIAR PARTY DIP

WHILE WE ARE CALLING THIS A PARTY DIP, IT REALLY COULD BE A DELICIOUS AND HEALTHY MEAL OR A SIDE DISH PACKED WITH NUTRITION. IT CAN BE SERVED ON TORTILLAS, WITH CHIPS, OR JUST PLAIN. IT'S A FAMILY FAVORITE!

INGREDIENTS

DIP DRESSING

1/4 cup olive oil

2 teaspoons salt

1/2 teaspoon pepper

2 teaspoons cumin

1 teaspoon granulated garlic

1/4 teaspoon minced garlic

Juice from 1 lime

2 tablespoons chia seeds

SERVES 12

PARTY DIP

1 can (11 ounces) white shoepeg corn, drained

1 can (15 ounces) black-eyed peas, drained

1 can (15 ounces) black beans, drained and rinsed

6 Roma tomatoes, chopped

1/2 cup chopped cilantro

2 avocados

6 green onions, diced

1 1/2 cups cooked grain mixture (optional)—*see tip*

1 1/2 jalapenos, diced

1 Mix the dressing ingredients together in a bowl. Set aside.

2 In a separate bowl, mix the dip ingredients together. Then gently stir in the dressing.

3 If you let the dip sit for a little bit, the vegetables, rice, and beans will pick up more of the flavors from the dressing. Then serve!

TIP:

For the grain mixture in the recipe, we cooked 1 cup of brown rice, 1/4 cup of buckwheat, and 1/4 cup of well-rinsed quinoa in 4 cups of water. Using a grain mixture in this recipe is optional, but the addition of grains tastes great, makes the meal go further, and gives the dip more nutritional balance.

VEGETABLE LENTIL SALAD

ENJOYING THIS SALAD IS A GREAT WAY TO EAT A LOT OF VEGETABLES. I ALSO LOVE THAT IT'S SO COLORFUL. WHEN YOU EAT A RAINBOW OF COLORS, YOU KNOW YOU ARE GETTING A NICE VARIETY OF NUTRIENTS. YOU ALSO GET AN ADDED BONUS OF LENTILS, CHIA, AND QUINOA—A BOOST OF PROTEIN—IN THIS SALAD.

1 Toss all the ingredients together in a bowl except the lime juice, salt, pepper, and chili powder.

2 In a separate small bowl, combine the lime juice, salt, pepper, and chili powder. Stir the mixture together and toss with the vegetables until the salad is covered.

3 Serve immediately for best results, or store in an airtight container in the refrigerator until ready to serve.

INGREDIENTS

1 cup cooked lentils

1/3 cup well-rinsed and cooked red quinoa

1/3 cup chia seeds

1/4 cup chopped purple onion

1 sweet potato, cooked and cubed

1/4 cup chopped yellow pepper

1/4 cup chopped red pepper

1/2 cup chopped zucchini

1/2 cup chopped avocado

2 Roma tomatoes, chopped

1/4 cup diced cilantro

Juice from one lime

1 teaspoon salt

1/4 teaspoon ground pepper

1/4 teaspoon chili powder

TIP:

We have a nice hand chopper that cubes the vegetables, which makes a salad like this incredibly easy to prepare. You can find it or something similar at any store that carries kitchen tools.

SERVES 6

MANGO DRESSING
ON TOSSED SALAD

I LOVE THE NATURAL SWEETNESS OF MANGOES, SO THEY ARE A PERFECT CHOICE FOR THIS DRESSING. CHIA ADDS A BOOST OF PROTEIN AND ALSO WORKS AS A NICE THICKENER.

INGREDIENTS

DRESSING

1 cup chopped mangoes

1/2 cup water

1 teaspoon apple cider vinegar

1 tablespoon olive oil

1/4 teaspoon salt

1/8 teaspoon cayenne pepper

1 tablespoon honey

2 tablespoons chia seeds

SALAD

4 cups spinach

1 cup chopped broccoli

1/2 cup dried cherries

1/2 cup dried apricots

4 green onions, chopped

4 stalks celery, chopped

1/2 cup diced carrots

Sunflower seeds, pumpkin seeds, or both

Feta cheese (optional)

1 Combine the dressing ingredients in a blender and pulse until smooth. Chill the dressing in the refrigerator while you make the salad.

2 Toss all the salad ingredients together in a bowl and serve with the dressing.

SERVES 6

CARROTS AND LEEKS

SOMETIMES WE FIND OURSELVES MORE MOTIVATED TO EAT VEGETABLES WHEN WE PUT MORE EFFORT INTO THE PREPARATION OF THEM. THE COMBINATION OF THE ORANGE AND THE HONEY MAKE THIS A WONDERFUL AFTERNOON SNACK.

1 In a saucepan, add the water and salt. Bring the water to a boil on medium heat.

2 Add the carrots and leek and cook for 4 minutes. While the vegetables are cooking, mix together the juice, honey, thyme, and chia in a small bowl—that is your dressing.

3 Drain the water from the saucepan and add the dressing. Toss the vegetables until they are completely covered. Garnish with orange zest. The vegetables are best when enjoyed warm.

INGREDIENTS

4 cups water

1 teaspoon salt

6 carrots, sliced into 1/4-inch pieces

1 leek, sliced

1/3 cup orange juice

1 tablespoon honey

1/2 teaspoon thyme

2 tablespoons chia seeds

Orange zest for garnish

SERVES 4–6

DID YOU KNOW?

Chia's high oil content tends to repel insects, so there's usually no need for pesticides when cultivating chia. It is truly organic and natural!

SWEET POTATO FRIES

SWEET POTATOES ARE LOADED WITH GREAT NUTRIENTS, AND WHEN YOU ADD CHIA, YOU REALLY HAVE A NUTRITIONAL POWERHOUSE. THESE FRIES HAVE GREAT FLAVOR, AND YOU CAN ENJOY THEM TOTALLY GUILT-FREE!

INGREDIENTS

2 sweet potatoes

1 teaspoon salt

1/2 teaspoon garlic powder

1/2 teaspoon paprika

1 tablespoon chia seeds

3 tablespoons water

2 tablespoons olive oil

SERVES 6

1 Wash the sweet potatoes, peel them, and cut them into strips that are about 1/4 inch thick.

2 Place the sweet potato strips in a large bowl and fill the rest of the bowl with ice water. Let the potatoes sit in the bowl for 30 minutes.

3 Mix together the salt, garlic powder, and paprika in a separate bowl. Grind the chia seeds and add the powder to the spices.

4 Stir the water and oil into the spices until well mixed. It will turn into a gelatinous mixture.

5 Preheat oven to 450 degrees. Remove the sweet potato strips from the ice bath and dry them thoroughly.

6 Line two cookie sheets with parchment paper and place the sweet potatoes on them. Pour the spice mixture over the fries and toss the fries with your fingers until the spice mixture evenly coats them.

7 Arrange the fries so that they don't touch each other and place the pans in the oven. Bake for 35 minutes or until the outsides are slightly crispy. (Baking time may vary depending on your oven and how thickly the fries were cut, so use your discretion.) Remove fries from the oven and serve immediately.

APPLE CHERRY SALAD

I LOVE WHEN I CAN ENJOY A SALAD WITH VERY LITTLE DRESSING—THAT WAY, I CAN ENJOY JUST THE NATURAL SWEETNESS OF THE VEGETABLES AND FRUIT. THIS IS ONE OF THOSE SALADS.

1 Combine the apples, celery, and cherries or cranberries in a bowl.

2 Pour the juice evenly over the fruit. Stir to mix.

3 Sprinkle the chia and drizzle the honey on top. Toss until all ingredients are mixed.

4 Garnish with more dried fruit, if desired, and serve.

INGREDIENTS

2 apples, chopped

4 stalks celery, chopped

1/4 cup dried cherries or cranberries

Juice from 2 oranges

1 tablespoon chia seeds

2 tablespoons honey

Extra dried cherries or cranberries for garnish

SERVES 4

TIP:

For this recipe, we like to use sweet, crisp apples. Honeycrisp, Gala, McIntosh, or Cortland apples work well.

MAIN DISHES

HONEY SALMON
WITH SPICY RUB

THE SWEET AND SPICY COMBINATION IN THIS SALMON RUB MAKES A DELICIOUS MEAL. IT DOESN'T TAKE LONG TO PREP, AND IT IS WELL WORTH THE EFFORT. THE CHIA IN THE RUB GIVES IT ADDED NUTRITION, TOO.

INGREDIENTS

SPICY RUB

1 tablespoon chili powder

1 teaspoon ground cumin

1/4 teaspoon salt

1/4 teaspoon freshly ground pepper

2 tablespoons chia seeds

SALMON

4 salmon fillets (5 ounces each)

2–3 tablespoons olive oil for coating salmon fillets

2 tablespoons coconut oil or olive oil

1 tablespoon honey

MAKES 4 FILLETS

1 Pour all of the rub ingredients except the chia into a bowl and stir. Blend the chia in a small chopper until it is powdery and stir it into the rub.

2 Brush 2–3 tablespoons of olive oil onto the salmon fillets.

3 Pour some of the rub onto a dinner plate and press a salmon fillet into it. Turn the fillet over on its other side and press until it is coated. Repeat the same process with the other fillets.

4 Heat a large skillet on medium heat. Pour in the coconut oil or olive oil and honey and stir until melted.

5 Place the fillets in the skillet and cook on both sides until cooked all the way through. Remove the fillets from the pan and put any extra rub that fell off in the pan back on top of the cooked fillets.

6 Serve while warm. This dish would pair great with a green salad and some brown rice.

TIP:

To grind up the chia for this recipe, Mom uses a small Black and Decker® coffee grinder. It works great for flaxseed, too.

CHICKEN SALAD
WITH CHIA DRESSING

CHIA SUBSTITUTES EASILY IN ANY RECIPE THAT CALLS FOR POPPY SEEDS. SALAD DRESSINGS ARE NO EXCEPTION. IF YOU LIKE POPPY SEED DRESSING ON YOUR SALADS, YOU WILL LOVE CHIA SEED DRESSINGS. CHIA THICKENS THE DRESSING AND ADDS AN EXTRA PUNCH OF OMEGA-3S.

1 Toss all of the salad ingredients except the bacon together in a large bowl.

2 In a separate bowl, whisk together the dressing ingredients.

3 Just prior to serving, top the salad with the dressing and the optional bacon.

INGREDIENTS

SALAD

2 cups grilled chicken, chopped into small pieces

1/2 cup chopped carrots

1/4–1/2 purple onion, diced

1 cucumber, sliced

4 cups spring salad greens mix (or other greens)

Bacon pieces for topping (optional)

DRESSING

1 cup plain yogurt

2–3 tablespoons honey or alternative sweetener

2–2 1/2 tablespoons lemon juice

1–2 teaspoons chia seeds

SERVES 4

STUFFED MEXICAN MINI PEPPERS
WITH QUINOA

THIS RECIPE MAKES A GREAT MAIN DISH, SNACK, SIDE DISH, OR APPETIZER. AND THE COLORS MAKE A BEAUTIFUL PRESENTATION. MOM ENJOYED THE CRUNCH OF EATING THE PEPPERS RAW, BUT YOU CAN COOK THEM IF YOU PREFER.

1 Preheat oven to 350 degrees if you plan to cook the peppers. Place a skillet on the stove on medium heat. Pour in the oil and heat it up.

2 Add the onion and garlic to the skillet and stir. Sauté until they start to turn a light golden color. Stir in the chia and cook for 2 minutes.

3 Stir in the quinoa, rice, salt, cumin, chili powder, and optional cheese. Cook until the mixture is warm throughout.

4 While the stuffing is cooking, cut a slit lengthwise in the peppers and use a small spoon to scoop out the seeds.

5 When the stuffing is warm, remove it from heat and mix in the cilantro.

6 Use a small spoon to stuff the mixture into the peppers. If you want to leave the peppers raw, omit step 7 and serve.

7 If you want to cook the peppers, place them on a greased baking sheet. Bake for 15–18 minutes until soft. Take the baking sheet out of the oven and let the peppers cool.

8 Serve when the pepper shells have cooled. The peppers are best when the filling is still warm. Store leftovers in an airtight container in the refrigerator.

INGREDIENTS

3–4 tablespoons olive oil

1/4 onion, chopped

2 cloves garlic, minced

4 tablespoons chia seeds

2/3 cup cooked quinoa

2/3 cup cooked brown rice

1/2 teaspoon salt

1/4 teaspoon cumin

1/4 teaspoon chili powder

1/4 cup shredded cheese (optional)

Handful of cilantro

12 mini peppers

SERVES 12

SWEET POTATO SKILLET

SWEET POTATOES ARE A WONDERFUL ADDITION TO ANY DISH—ESPECIALLY THIS ONE. THEY ADD COLOR, NUTRITION, AND NATURAL SWEETNESS. MOM FINDS THEM TO BE A HEALTHY AND DELICIOUS SUPPLEMENT TO ANY MEAL.

INGREDIENTS

2 tablespoons olive oil

2 cloves garlic, minced

1 onion, diced

1 bell pepper, chopped

1/4 cup chia seeds

3 chicken breasts, cooked and chopped

2 sweet potatoes, cooked and cubed

3 cups cooked brown rice

1/2 teaspoon thyme

1 teaspoon salt

1/4 teaspoon pepper

SERVES 6

1 Warm a large skillet on medium heat and add the oil. Stir in the garlic and onion. Cook them together for 3–4 minutes or until the onion starts to soften.

2 Stir in the pepper and chia and cook for another 3–4 minutes.

3 Add the chicken, potatoes, rice, thyme, salt, and pepper. Cover the mixture and cook for about 10 minutes on medium-low heat, letting the flavors meld together, and stirring a couple of times. Don't overstir, or the mixture will get mushy. Add 1/4 cup of water if the mixture needs more moisture.

4 Serve while warm.

PARMESAN-CRUSTED CHICKEN

CHIA CAN BE USED AS AN EGG SUBSTITUTE IN MANY RECIPES, AS IT IS IN THIS ONE. INSTEAD OF DIPPING CHICKEN IN EGG TO HELP THE BREAD CRUMBS AND SEASONING STICK, WE USE A CHIA GEL.

1 Preheat oven to 350 degrees. Grease a baking sheet.

2 Cut the chicken into strips. Set strips aside.

3 Mix together the ground chia and water until it makes a thick gel. Place the gel mixture in the refrigerator for 10 minutes.

4 Combine the bread crumbs, cheese, salt, and dry mustard in a shallow dish.

5 Add the milk to the chia mixture and stir until combined.

6 Dip the chicken strips into the chia mixture and then roll in the bread crumb mixture. Place the coated strips on the prepared baking sheet.

7 Bake for 35 minutes or until the chicken is done.

INGREDIENTS

3 boneless, skinless chicken breasts

1 tablespoon chia, ground

4 tablespoons water

1 cup whole grain bread crumbs

1/2 cup finely grated Parmesan cheese

1/2 tablespoon salt

1 teaspoon dry mustard

1/4 cup milk

SERVES 4

DID YOU KNOW?

The Aztec people used chia for its medicinal properties, particularly to help heal skin conditions and relieve joint pain. Even today, some people believe that chia may have anti-inflammatory benefits for arthritis patients.

DESSERTS

VANILLA CHIA PUDDING

I AM A BIG FAN OF BOTH TAPIOCA AND RICE PUDDING, AND THIS TREAT REMINDS ME OF A COMBINATION OF THEM. THIS PUDDING IS QUICK AND EASY TO MAKE, AND IT WOULD BE A GREAT BREAKFAST, SNACK, OR DESSERT. YOU CAN ENJOY IT AS SOFT SERVE AFTER COOLING IT FOR AN HOUR, OR YOU CAN CHILL IT FOR FOUR HOURS OR OVERNIGHT FOR A THICKER PUDDING. WE LOVED EVERY BITE OF IT!

INGREDIENTS

1/2 cup canned coconut milk (full fat)

1 cup unsweetened vanilla almond milk

2 tablespoons maple syrup

1/4 cup chia seeds

1 cup fresh (or frozen and thawed) raspberries

SERVES 2

1 In a mason jar, combine the coconut milk, almond milk, syrup, and chia. Put on the lid and shake the jar several times to evenly distribute the seeds.

2 Place the covered jar in the refrigerator for 30 minutes.

3 Take the jar out of the refrigerator and shake or stir. Cover again and place back in the refrigerator. It will be ready to eat as soft serve after another 30 minutes of refrigeration. If you want it to be thicker, wait at least 4 hours or chill overnight.

4 Once the pudding has reached your desired consistency, top with the raspberries and devour.

RAW BROWNIE BITES

THESE ARE DELICIOUS BROWNIES WITHOUT THE USUAL GUILT. YOU CAN HAVE THEM READY IN THE REFRIGERATOR FOR WHEN YOU NEED A SWEET FIX, AND THEY ARE EASY TO MAKE! MAKE YOUR OWN ALMOND BUTTER USING THE RECIPE ON PAGE 124.

INGREDIENTS

1/4 cup almond milk

3 tablespoons chia seeds

2 1/2 tablespoons cocoa powder

1 tablespoon honey

1 tablespoon coconut oil

1 teaspoon vanilla

1/2 cup cashew butter or almond butter

1/4 cup cashews, chopped

MAKES ABOUT 8 BITES

1 In a blender, pulse the milk and chia together until the seeds are broken down.

2 Add the cocoa, honey, oil, vanilla, and nut butter. Blend and stir until all ingredients are combined. The mixture will be sticky.

3 Place the mixture in the refrigerator for about 30 minutes or until thick.

4 Place the chopped cashews on a plate. Grease hands with a small amount of oil.

5 Roll the brownie mixture into 1-inch balls. Then roll the balls in the chopped cashews.

6 Enjoy immediately or store in an airtight container in the refrigerator.

ALMOND PUDDING

THIS PUDDING HAS A TEXTURE SIMILAR TO TAPIOCA PUDDING. WE SOMETIMES ADD A TABLESPOON OF COCOA AND CHANGE THE ALMOND EXTRACT TO A TABLESPOON OF VANILLA EXTRACT TO MAKE IT CHOCOLATE PUDDING INSTEAD.

1 Stir all ingredients together in a bowl and place in the refrigerator. The mixture will start to gel in 10–15 minutes. Leave in the refrigerator until chilled through, about an hour.

2 When mixture is chilled, serve and enjoy.

INGREDIENTS

1/2 cup chia seeds

2 cups almond coconut milk

1 teaspoon almond extract

1/2 teaspoon cinnamon (optional)

Fruit, milk, or honey for toppings

SERVES 4

CHOCOLATE PEANUT BUTTER PUDDING

WE THINK EVERY DAY IS A GREAT DAY TO ENJOY PUDDING, ESPECIALLY WHEN YOU USE A HEALTHY RECIPE LIKE THIS ONE. YOU CAN'T GO WRONG WHEN YOU COMBINE CHOCOLATE AND PEANUT BUTTER!

INGREDIENTS

2 cups unsweetened vanilla almond milk

3 tablespoons honey or 6 softened dates

4 tablespoons chia seeds

2 tablespoons natural creamy peanut butter

2 tablespoons cocoa powder

1 banana, chopped and frozen

SERVES 4

1 Combine all ingredients in a blender in the order listed. Pulse until smooth.

2 Pour the mixture into dishes and chill in the refrigerator for at least 4 hours or overnight.

3 When chilled, remove the mixture from the refrigerator and serve.

TIP:

To soften the dates, soak them in water for about an hour. They are a great sugar substitute in this recipe.

CHOCOLATE CHIP CHUNK BARS

WHAT IS FASTER TO MAKE THAN COOKIES? COOKIE BARS! AND THESE COOKIES PACK A PUNCH OF WHOLE GRAINS, MAKING THEM MUCH HEALTHIER THAN YOUR AVERAGE SWEET SNACK.

INGREDIENTS

- 3/4 cup coconut oil
- 3/4 cup honey
- 2 eggs
- 1/3 cup chia seeds
- 1 teaspoon vanilla
- 2 cups old-fashioned oats
- 1 cup whole grain flour (we used Kamut®)
- 3/4 teaspoon baking soda
- 1/4 teaspoon salt
- 1 cup dark chocolate chips (70 percent cocoa or greater)

SERVES 9

1 Preheat oven to 350 degrees. In a medium bowl, beat together the oil and honey. Then beat in the eggs one at a time.

2 Stir in the chia and vanilla.

3 In a separate large mixing bowl, combine the oats, flour, baking soda, and salt.

4 Add the wet ingredients to the dry ingredients and mix until just combined. Then fold in the chocolate chips.

5 Scoop the dough into a 9 x 9–inch pan and spread out the batter until smooth.

6 Place the pan in the heated oven and bake for 25–30 minutes.

7 Take the pan out of the oven and let cool. Cut into 3-inch squares and enjoy!

CHOCOLATE BANANA CREAM PUDDING

MY FAMILY HAS ALWAYS ENJOYED CHOCOLATE PUDDING WITH BANANAS. THIS IS A HEALTHY WAY TO MAKE CHOCOLATE PUDDING WITHOUT HAVING TO COOK ANYTHING OR ADD MUCH SWEETENER. IT'S CREAMY AND YUMMY, AND THE CHIA THICKENS IT NICELY.

1 In a blender, mix the milk, honey or vegan sweetener, cocoa, and frozen bananas until smooth. Then add the chia and blend until mixture is smooth.

2 Pour mixture into serving dishes. Chill for a couple hours in the refrigerator until pudding is as thick as you prefer.

3 If desired, serve topped with chopped, fresh banana.

INGREDIENTS

1 can (14 ounces) coconut milk (full fat)

4 tablespoons honey or vegan sweetener

2 tablespoons cocoa powder

2 bananas, chopped and frozen

2 tablespoons chia seeds, ground

1 fresh banana, chopped (optional)

SERVES 2

SPREADS & SAUCES

RASPBERRY CHIA JAM

WE LOVE BEING ABLE TO ENJOY RASPBERRIES ALL YEAR LONG THROUGH FROZEN JAM. (THOUGH FEEL FREE TO SUBSTITUTE ANY KIND OF BERRY FOR RASPBERRIES IN THIS RECIPE TO MAKE DIFFERENT TYPES OF JAM.) STORE-BOUGHT JAM JUST DOESN'T CAPTURE THE SAME GREAT FLAVOR. THE BEST THING ABOUT THIS RECIPE IS THAT YOU DON'T COOK THE BERRIES, SO THEY TASTE REALLY FRESH. ALSO, THE CHIA IS A PERFECT THICKENER.

INGREDIENTS

1 pound of fresh or frozen raspberries

2 1/2 tablespoons chia seeds

3 tablespoons honey (or more if you want the jam to be sweeter)

MAKES 3/4–1 CUP OF JAM

1 In a blender, pulse the berries, leaving them slightly chunky. Pulse more if you prefer a smoother consistency.

2 Add the chia and honey and pulse a couple more times.

3 Pour the jam into airtight containers that are freezer safe and put in the freezer. Leave a little room on top for expansion.

4 When ready to use, take out of the freezer and enjoy.

BANANA RASPBERRY SWIRL

Use your raspberry chia jam in this refreshing dessert! It is a tasty, guilt-free treat that whips up in minutes and is even dairy-free. It's so easy to make and oh so good. Mom says she can never have too many raspberries, and the beauty is that they are great for you.

1 banana, chopped and frozen
4 tablespoons raspberry chia jam

Blend and pulse the banana until smooth. Scoop blended banana into a dish, swirl in the raspberry jam, and enjoy.

ALMOND BUTTER

WE LOVE ALMOND BUTTER. FEEL FREE TO USE IT ANYWHERE YOU WOULD USE PEANUT BUTTER. IT'S RELATIVELY EASY TO MAKE AND HAS MORE NUTRITION THAN PEANUT BUTTER, ESPECIALLY WITH THE ADDED CHIA.

INGREDIENTS

1 tablespoon coconut oil

1 tablespoon honey or maple syrup

1 cup almonds

1 1/2 tablespoons chia seeds

MAKES 3/4 CUP

1 Combine all ingredients in a blender or food processor in the order listed. Blend and pulse until smooth.

2 Serve immediately or store in an airtight container in the refrigerator until ready to use.

ROASTED PEPPER PESTO

THIS IS NOT IN ANY WAY A TRADITIONAL PESTO, BUT YOU CAN USE IT IN THE SAME WAY THAT YOU MIGHT USE A BASIL PESTO. WE THINK IT PAIRS WELL WITH SANDWICHES, CRACKERS, VEGETABLES, BAGUETTES, OR PASTA. THE JALAPEÑO GIVES IT A NICE KICK, TOO.

1. Preheat oven to 350 degrees. Cut the peppers in half and use a small spoon to scoop out the seeds. Lay the peppers facedown on a cookie sheet and place them in the oven. Roast the peppers for about 15 minutes. Flip them over to the other side and roast for another 15 minutes.

2. Take the peppers out of the oven, place them in a bowl, and cover the bowl with plastic wrap. Let the peppers steam for 10 minutes. Then peel off the skins. They should come off easily after steaming in the bowl.

3. Put the peppers into a blender and pulse until smooth. Then add the remaining ingredients and pulse again until smooth.

4. Serve pesto at once or store in an airtight container in the refrigerator.

INGREDIENTS

2 red or orange bell peppers

1/2 jalapeño, minced

2 cloves garlic, minced

1/2 teaspoon salt

1 tablespoon vinegar

1 tablespoon chia seeds

MAKES
3/4 CUP

ROASTED RED PEPPER HUMMUS

WE LOVE MAKING OUR OWN HUMMUS. THIS RECIPE IS A FAVORITE AT FAMILY GATHERINGS BECAUSE OF ITS GREAT FLAVOR—THE BOWL GETS SCRAPED CLEAN!

INGREDIENTS

2 red bell peppers

1 teaspoon plus 2 tablespoons olive oil

1/4 onion, diced

5 tablespoons freshly squeezed lemon juice

1/4 cup tahini

2 cloves garlic, minced

3/4 teaspoon cumin

Pinch of cayenne pepper

1 teaspoon salt

3 tablespoons chia seeds

1 can (15 ounces) garbanzo beans, drained and rinsed

MAKES 1 1/2 CUPS

1 Preheat oven to broil. Cut the peppers in half and remove the seeds. Place peppers skin side up on a cookie sheet. Broil for 5–10 minutes until the skin is slightly charred. Watch closely to prevent the peppers from burning.

2 Immediately place the peppers in a bowl and cover with plastic wrap. Let the peppers steam for 10 minutes.

3 When the peppers have cooled down and are ready to handle, uncover the bowl and peel the skins off the peppers. They should come off easily after steaming in the bowl. Then chop the peppers.

4 In a small skillet, heat 1 teaspoon of the olive oil. Sauté the onion for 3–5 minutes or until tender. Remove from heat.

5 In a food processor or blender, pulse the lemon juice and tahini for about 30 seconds until creamy. Add the garlic, the remaining 2 tablespoons of olive oil, cumin, cayenne pepper, salt, chia, and sautéed onions. Continue blending, scraping the edges of the blender until the mixture is creamy.

6 Pour in half the beans and blend until smooth. Add the remaining beans and blend again until smooth. Finally, add the peppers to the blender or food processor and blend until the mixture is smooth.

7 Serve immediately with chips, vegetables, or your favorite snack to dip into hummus. Store in an airtight container in the refrigerator. The hummus can last up to a week.

CHIA LEMON DRESSING

WITH THE TANG OF LEMON JUICE AND THE SWEETNESS OF HONEY, WE THINK THIS DRESSING IS A REFRESHING ADDITION TO A GREEN SALAD.

INGREDIENTS

2 tablespoons lemon juice

1/2 teaspoon vinegar

1/4 cup olive oil

1 tablespoon honey

1/2 teaspoon salt

1/8 teaspoon pepper

1 tablespoon chia seeds

**MAKES
1/2 CUP**

1 Pour all the ingredients into a blender in the order listed and pulse until combined, about 1–2 minutes.

2 Serve immediately or store in an airtight container in the refrigerator until ready to use. Stir with a wire whisk or blend in a blender before serving.

CREAMY CHIA DRESSING

CREAMY DRESSINGS ARE DELICIOUS, BUT THEY USUALLY COME AT A COST: ULTIMATELY, OUR HEALTH. THIS ONE IS BOTH DELICIOUS *AND* HEALTHY!

....

1 Pour all ingredients into a blender and pulse until smooth, about 1–2 minutes.

2 Serve dressing immediately or store in airtight container in the refrigerator until ready to use. If the dressing thickens too much after being in the refrigerator, stir in 1–2 tablespoons of water to thin it out.

INGREDIENTS

....

1/4 cup plain yogurt

1/8 cup olive oil

3 tablespoons honey

2 tablespoons vinegar

1/4 teaspoon garlic powder

1/4 teaspoon salt

1/4 teaspoon dry mustard

1 tablespoon chia seeds

MAKES ABOUT 1 CUP

DID YOU KNOW?

Though chia doesn't have a distinctive scent, it originates from the mint family.

Volume Measurements

U.S.	METRIC
1 teaspoon	5 milliliters
1 tablespoon	15 milliliters
1/4 cup	60 milliliters
1/3 cup	75 milliliters
1/2 cup	125 milliliters
2/3 cup	150 milliliters
3/4 cup	175 milliliters
1 cup	250 milliliters

Weight Measurements

U.S.	METRIC
1/2 ounce	15 grams
1 ounce	30 grams
3 ounces	90 grams
4 ounces	115 grams
8 ounces	225 grams
12 ounces	350 grams
1 pound	450 grams
2 1/4 pounds	1 kilogram

Temperature Conversion

FAHRENHEIT	CELSIUS
250	120
300	150
325	160
350	180
375	190
400	200
425	220
450	230

ABOUT FAMILIUS

Welcome to a place where mothers and fathers are celebrated, not belittled. Where values are at the core of happy family life. Where boo-boos are still kissed, cake beaters are still licked, and mistakes are still okay. Welcome to a place where books—and family—are beautiful. Familius: a book publisher dedicated to helping families be happy.

VISIT OUR WEBSITE: WWW.FAMILIUS.COM

Our website is a different kind of place. Get inspired, read articles, discover books, watch videos, connect with our family experts, download books and apps and audiobooks, and along the way, discover how values and happy family life go together.

JOIN OUR FAMILY

There are lots of ways to connect with us! Subscribe to our newsletters at www.familius.com to receive uplifting daily inspiration, essays from our Pater Familius, a free ebook every month, and the first word on special discounts and Familius news.

BECOME AN EXPERT

Familius authors and other established writers interested in helping families be happy are invited to join our family and contribute online content. If you have something important to say on the family, join our expert community by applying at:

www.familius.com/apply-to-become-a-familius-expert

GET BULK DISCOUNTS

If you feel a few friends and family might benefit from what you've read, let us know and we'll be happy to provide you with quantity discounts. Simply email us at specialorders@familius.com.

Website: www.familius.com
Facebook: www.facebook.com/paterfamilius
Twitter: @familiustalk, @paterfamilius1
Pinterest: www.pinterest.com/familius

THE MOST IMPORTANT WORK YOU EVER DO WILL BE WITHIN THE WALLS OF YOUR OWN HOME.